SACRED PLACES S

Sacred Argyll and Clyde

SCOTLAND'S CHURCHES SCHEME

SAINT ANDREW PRESS
Edinburgh

First published in 2011 by
SAINT ANDREW PRESS
121 George Street
Edinburgh EH2 4YN

The cover photograph is of Iona Abbey © RCAHMS

ISBN 978 0 7152 0957 8

British Library Cataloguing in Publication Data
A catalogue record for this book is available from the British Library.

It is the publisher's policy to only use papers that are natural and recyclable and that
have been manufactured from timber grown in renewable, properly managed forests.
All of the manufacturing processes of the papers are expected to conform to the
environmental regulations of the country of origin.

Typeset in Enigma by Waverley Typesetters, Warham, Norfolk
Manufactured in Great Britain by Bell & Bain Ltd, Glasgow

Sacred Argyll and Clyde

BUCKINGHAM PALACE

As Patron of Scotland's Churches Scheme, I warmly welcome this publication as part of the *Sacred Places* series of books being produced by the Scheme.

The story of the heritage and culture of Scotland would be lacking significantly without a strong focus on its churches and sacred sites. I am sure that this guidebook will be a source of information and enjoyment both to the people of Scotland and to our visitors.

Anne

Scotland's Churches Scheme

www.sacredscotland.org.uk

Scotland's Churches Scheme is an ecumenical charitable trust, providing an opportunity to access the nation's living heritage of faith by assisting the 'living' churches in membership to:

- Promote spiritual understanding by enabling the public to appreciate all buildings designed for worship and active as living churches
- Work together with others to make the Church the focus of the community
- Open their doors with a welcoming presence
- Tell the story of the building (however old or new), its purpose and heritage (artistic, architectural and historical)
- Provide information for visitors, young and old

The Scheme has grown rapidly since its inception in 1994, and there are now more than 1,200 churches in membership. These churches are to be found across all parts of Scotland and within all the denominations.

The *Sacred Scotland* theme promoted by Scotland's Churches Scheme focuses on the wish of both visitors and local communities to be able to access our wonderful range of church buildings in a meaningful way, whether the visit be occasioned by spiritual or heritage motivation or both. The Scheme can advise and assist member churches on visitor welcome, and, with its range of 'how-to' brochures, provide information on research, presentation, security and other live issues relating to the buildings and associated graveyards. With its network of local representatives, the Scheme encourages the opening of doors and the care of tourists and locals alike, and offers specific services such as the provision of grants for organ-playing.

Sacred Scotland (www.sacredscotland.org.uk), the website of Scotland's Churches Scheme, opens the door to Scotland's story by exploring living traditions of faith in city, town, village and island across the country. The site is a portal to access information on Scotland's churches of all denominations and is a starting point for your special journeys.

The Scheme has also embarked, with support from Scottish Enterprise and Historic Scotland, on the identification and promotion of Scotland's Pilgrim Ways, with the huge resource of its expanding website and database of sacred sites. With the growing awareness and enthusiasm for such an initiative, a pilot project is already under way and is seen as a welcome development of the Scheme's existing activity and publications.

We are delighted to be working with Saint Andrew Press in the publication of this *Sacred Places* series of regional guides to Scotland's churches. In 2009, the first three volumes were published – *Sacred South-West Scotland*; *Sacred Edinburgh and Midlothian*; and *Sacred Fife and the Forth Valley*. In 2010, a further three volumes were published – *Sacred Borders and East Lothian*; *Sacred Glasgow and the Clyde Valley*; and *Sacred North-East Scotland*. This volume, *Sacred Argyll and Clyde*, is one of the final three to be published in 2011, now covering the whole country. The others are *Sacred Highlands and Islands* and *Sacred Perthshire and the Tay Valley*. We are grateful to the authors of the introductory articles, Professor John Hume, one of our trustees, and Marian Pallister, for their expert contributions to our understanding of sacred places.

The growth of 'spiritual tourism' worldwide is reflected in the million-plus people who visit Scotland's religious sites annually. We hope that the information in this book will be useful in bringing alive the heritage as well as the ministry of welcome which our churches offer. In the words of our former President, Lady Marion Fraser: 'we all owe a deep debt of gratitude to the many people of vision who work hard and imaginatively to create a lasting and peaceful atmosphere which you will carry away with you as a special memory when you leave'.

Dr Brian Fraser
Director, Scotland's Churches Scheme
Dunedin, Holehouse Road, Eaglesham, Glasgow G76 0JF

Scotland's Churches Scheme: local representatives
Mrs Ann Moohan (*Renfrewshire*)
Mr Ian Milne (*Inverclyde*)
Rev. James MacFarlane (*Argyll and Bute*)
Mr John Gair (*West Dunbartonshire*)

Invitation to Pilgrimage

Argyll and Clyde

The western fringe of Scotland, known today as Argyll and the Isles, has been populated for at least 8,000 years. There is evidence that, for six of those eight millennia, there has been for some a sacred purpose in travelling to the area. Our prehistory is punctuated by standing stones, henges, elaborate chambered cairns and complex rock carvings. Experts suggest that many of these sites could have had a religious purpose. Some of the standing stones, for instance, line up with the setting sun at the times of the winter and summer solstices. The land and seascapes hold a mystic charm that encourages the idea of *Tir nan Og* – the land of eternal youth; a Celtic heaven beyond the watery horizon.

The pilgrim has never been a stranger to Argyll and the Isles. When the early saints came here from Ireland – Brendan and Columba are my own personal favourites – they were not above employing the kind of inculturation seen today in Africa and other developing areas of the world, using the symbols of the Druids to pull adherents of an earlier religion into Christianity.

Brendan and Columba and their confreres gently converted the Pictish settlers to one God and not many; to believe in a crucified and risen Christ and a Holy Spirit. St Patrick's concept of Christ within, above, before, behind – an all-enveloping, guiding and guarding presence – came with these Celts from Ireland in the sixth century.

Around AD 542, Brendan the Navigator (they say he may even have reached America in a tiny coracle) founded a monastery on Eileach an Naoimh, the most southerly of the Garvellach islands in the Firth of Lorn. Some of the beehive cells are still almost intact; and the tiny roofless chapel may provide us with the oldest church building in what are now the British Isles.

Be that as it may, St Brendan's monastery sends out a powerful invitation to pilgrimage. It was a call we answered with Fr Michael Hutson when he was parish priest at St Margaret's Catholic Church in Lochgilphead. We sailed on a catamaran and another small craft from Crinan Ferry, experienced the most beautiful, simple Mass in the ruins of the chapel, and shared a parish picnic in the company of Celtic spirits from sixteen centuries ago. St Columba's mother, Eithne, is said to have been buried on this island – a spot as near to *Tir nan Og* as a Christian burial will allow.

Of course, we fall over ancient chapels in this part of the world. The prefix 'kil' gives the clue: Kilmartin, Kilmichael, Kilbride, Kilmore, Kilmory, Kilberry – the list goes on and on, and each one indicates that a modern village was once the site (or perhaps still is) of a medieval chapel or of an even older holy place.

Although the parish church in Kilmartin was built in 1835, the name and the thirteenth-century grave-slabs in the churchyard are evidence of a faith stretching back through the centuries. If one were to accept an invitation to make a pilgrimage to this part of Argyll and the Isles, however, one must also go next door to Kilmartin House Museum, which temporarily houses the Kilmichael Cross.

Kilmichael was a seat of ecclesiastical power from the Middle Ages. When the Reformation swept through Scotland in the 1560s, Kilmichael's ancient church did not escape. Someone, however, drew back from the iconoclasm that saw 'Papist' artefacts smashed to smithereens or thrown into rivers and the sea from Campbeltown to Stornoway. A thirteenth-century carved stone cross was preserved as a door lintel and discovered in 1827 when the old church came down and a new one was built.

The village was then on the fringe of a huge estate owned by the Malcolm family. Their blacksmith took the broken cross to the village of Bellanoch and fixed it with iron bars. It served for a while as the market cross in Kilmichael, still the site of a major cattle market. Then, in the 1840s, the Malcolms built a new mansion house with a little Episcopal chapel next door. They scooped up the Kilmichael Cross and planted it in the grounds of the chapel. It stayed there for over 150 years until the current incumbent, Robin Malcolm, saw how badly it was deteriorating. Funding was sought for expert repair; and this beautiful cross, with an almost Norse-style Christ crucified still miraculously intact, now awaits its final home – in Kilmichael's parish church, it is to be hoped.

The Norsemen, of course, destroyed the abbey on the island of Iona, where Columba established his monastery. The restored building now attracts people of faith and people of none, and despite the crowds the sacred island of Iona still has a peace to offer the pilgrim. But so does Columba's cave in Knapdale, where the Episcopal minister at Christ Church in Lochgilphead leads a tiny pilgrimage to commemorate the saint's death on 9 June. So too does the modern Catholic cathedral of St Columba in Oban.

Some places just breathe the breath of God. It whispers still through the bustle of tourists on the Isle of Mull – Tobermory means 'Well of Mary'. It buffets the tip of the Tayvallich peninsula where the thirteenth-century Keills chapel silently bears witness to past expressions of faith. It can, very occasionally, be a balmy breeze fluttering around Cille Bharra – the ninth-century chapel of St Barr at Eoligarry on the Isle of Barra (Western Isles).

It is intriguing to think that, in medieval times, when the Norsemen ruled all of our islands, the parishioners were answerable to a bishop in Bergen, and many perhaps made pilgrimage to Trondheim's Nidaros cathedral, built in 1066 to shelter the body of St Olav.

Today, Argyll and the Isles themselves invite pilgrimage. Here we may follow the paths of Columba, Brendan or Barr to seek peace, a connection with God's earth, sea and sky, and an affirmation that Christ is indeed before us, behind us, within us.

MARIAN PALLISTER
Lochgilphead

Introduction

Sacred Argyll and Clyde

The area covered by this volume – Argyll and Bute, Inverclyde, Renfrewshire and West Dunbartonshire – is both scenically and culturally varied. It is divided by water, but was until the late modern period united by it. It was only in the second half of the twentieth century that shipping was ousted by road transport over much of the area. Even today, the area is largely dependent on ferry services from Inverclyde to Cowal and Bute, and from mainland Argyll to the Inner Hebrides. The principal cultural and religious influences have, therefore, been largely reliant on sea and river, with three-way traffic between this part of Scotland, Ireland, north-western England and Wales.

British, Scots-Irish and Norse influences all melded during the first millennium AD, with Christianity a powerful unifying force. The most celebrated Christian missionary in the area was St Columba, basing his mission on Iona – but there were many other missionary saints whose names are marked by church dedications, and by place names (including those beginning with 'Kil'). These are most numerous in Argyll and Bute, but are also found in other parts of our area. Much of Argyll and Bute is barely suitable for agriculture, so settlements were generally small and scattered. There was some fishing, but generally distance from markets limited its development to the nineteenth and early twentieth centuries.

The sheltered waters of the estuary and of the Firth of Clyde and its sea lochs were the nursery for the development of the steam-boat in the second decade of the nineteenth century. Steamers had a transforming

Fig. 1. Chapel, Dunstaffnage Castle, Argyll and Bute

Fig. 2. St Mahew's Roman Catholic Church, Cardross, Argyll and Bute

effect on the area, resulting in the development of holiday resorts and 'summer suburbs' along the coast of the Firth of Clyde, including Dunoon and Innellan, Rothesay and its suburbs, and strings of settlements along Loch Long, Gareloch, the Holy Loch and the Kyles of Bute, where the topography squeezes settlement into narrow coastal strips.

The historical prosperity of these areas has been dependent on industry, or on trade, rather than on agriculture. Urban settlements are comparatively rare over much of the area: Campbeltown, Tarbert, Lochgilphead, Inveraray, Oban, Dunoon and Helensburgh in Argyll; Rothesay on Bute. The large settlements are in Dunbartonshire and the old county of Renfrewshire: Dumbarton and its linear 'suburbs' on the River Leven; Clydebank and Dalmuir in West Dunbartonshire. Inverclyde has Gourock, Greenock and Port Glasgow, with the anomalous Kilmacolm an inland analogue of the select seaside suburbs of the Firth of Clyde. The only really sizeable place in the whole region is Paisley, one of the largest towns in Scotland, with its satellite towns of Renfrew and Johnstone. Bridge of Weir is largely another Kilmacolm.

The driver of economic and population growth in these eastern parts of the area was maritime trade, conducted mainly through Greenock and Port Glasgow, which created markets for local industries and supplied raw materials for new industries, of which the most important were reliant on cotton (and to a more limited extent on wool, silk and flax): spinning; weaving; bleaching, dyeing and calico-printing; and thread-making. Industries related to other imported materials were the tobacco trade and, more importantly, the sugar trade. Greenock's prosperity was for many years based largely on sugar-refining. Finally, there were the more directly maritime trades – obviously shipbuilding and marine engineering, less obviously rope- and sailmaking.

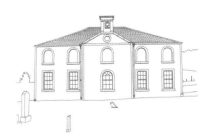

Fig. 3. North Knapdale Parish Church, Kilmichael of Inverlussa, Argyll and Bute

Fig. 4. The former Kilchoman Parish Church, Islay, Argyll and Bute

The shipbuilding and marine engineering industries were notable in Clydebank and Dalmuir, Greenock and Port Glasgow, Dumbarton and Dalreoch, and Paisley and Renfrew. Clydebank built the largest, Greenock and Port Glasgow the greatest tonnage, and Dumbarton the fastest ships. Paisley and Renfrew built more dredgers and other harbour craft than any others. Greenock built submarines, and Clydebank, Dalmuir and Greenock made battleships. The large-scale development of all of these industries was crammed into less than two centuries from the 1770s to the 1960s. Their collapse has resulted in the introduction of new industries, but also in widespread loss of confidence and in considerable urban deprivation. The early growth of Greenock, Port Glasgow and Paisley, from the seventeenth century, resulted in a high concentration of what became sub-standard housing, which was replaced from the 1930s by the development of peripheral housing estates. The destruction of much of central Greenock by German bombing in 1941 also stimulated urban renewal.

A distinctive feature of the Firth of Clyde was the establishment of linear settlements along the coastline, composed of 'marine villas', secondary homes for business families from the industrial areas of west central Scotland. This type of 'sub-urban' settlement became possible because of the perfection of a network of steamship services, which flourished from the early nineteenth century until after the Second World War. Many of the upper middle-class families who built marine villas also took up yachting, which flourished in the later nineteenth and early twentieth centuries, and which has again become a staple of the economy of Argyll since the 1960s. The steamers which made possible settlement along the Clyde littoral also encouraged the growth of day trips from places on the upper Clyde to what became 'resorts', such as Dunoon or Rothesay (and Largs and

Fig. 5. Ardchattan Parish Church, Argyll and Bute

Fig. 6. Garelochhead Parish Church, Argyll and Bute

Millport in what is now North Ayrshire). The day-trip market, complemented increasingly by holidaymaking in rented accommodation, resulted in the expansion of the permanent population of the resort towns. Wealthier holidaymakers also stimulated the growth of Oban, which became a notable centre for summer visitors to the western Highlands and the Inner Hebrides, popularised by Victorian writers and composers. The increasing industrialisation of central Scotland and the holiday trade of Argyll and Bute resulted in considerable migration of people (many Gaelic-speaking) out of the rural parts of Argyll and Bute, which were generally sparsely populated.

This socio-economic discussion is, I believe, helpful in understanding the pattern of church-building in the area. Places like Paisley, Port Glasgow, Greenock and Dumbarton have, or had, experiences comparable to those of other large central-belt settlements, with church buildings of all major, and some minor, denominations. Paisley and Greenock, in particular, have very complex church histories, largely on account of the wealth of sections of the population at different times. On the other hand, much of rural Argyll was never wealthy, and so most of its parish churches are relatively modest. The impact of the eighteenth-century Secessions and the Disruption of 1843 did not have an impact on our area comparable with that in the eastern Highlands and the Western Isles, though in Paisley the Secessions were successful. The immigration of Gaelic-speakers into the essentially Lowland towns of Greenock, Paisley and Campbeltown led, however, to the construction of Gaelic chapels, where migrants could worship in their own mellifluous language. Of other denominations, the most successful was arguably the

Fig. 7. The former Kilcalmonell Free Church, Clachan, Argyll and Bute

Fig. 8. Tobermory Parish Church, Mull, Argyll and Bute

Scottish Episcopal Church, with a cathedral in Oban (1863–1968, **45**) and numerous small churches scattered through the countryside as well as in the towns. Land-owners, many of whom had been educated in England, were largely responsible for the construction of Episcopal churches. Roman Catholicism was less widespread in its influence, largely because there was no significant legacy of 'Old Catholicism', and because the lack of economic opportunity in much of the area deterred large-scale immigration from Ireland. Only in the industrial towns of Renfrewshire, Dunbartonshire and Inverclyde were there significant Roman Catholic populations, almost all migrant. The construction of a Roman Catholic cathedral in Oban (1932–58, **46**) was largely prompted by the revival of 'Old Catholicism' in areas to the north and west of that town. In Inverclyde and Renfrewshire, minor Protestant denominations were unusually prominent. Methodists, Baptists and Congregationalists were all notable in the towns.

In this introduction, I have tried to draw common threads from the economic and social background of the area, but because of the marked differences between the local-authority areas included it makes sense to deal with their church buildings, as sacred spaces, separately. The order of areas in this introduction reflects that in the gazetteer: Argyll and Bute; Inverclyde; Renfrewshire; and West Dunbartonshire.

Argyll and Bute

Argyll is a very important area in the history of Christianity in Scotland, with the little island of Iona recognised as one of the major centres from which Christianity was spread throughout Scotland. Its position on the western seaboard and its links by sea with Ireland were important – as, too, was probably a pre-Christian sense of spirituality. The Gaelic heaven, 'Tir nan Og', the land of the ever young, was seen as being out to the west, beyond the setting sun, so that Iona, with no land to the west nearer than North America, could well have been seen as close to heaven. Be that as

Fig. 9. Oban Congregational Church,
Argyll and Bute

it may, the Irish-Celtic Church was an immensely powerful and persistent influence on Scotland. The many ruined chapels in Argyll are for the most part single-chambered buildings, implying no separation between clergy and laity. There are also remote places of retreat, such as the monastic site on Eileach an Naoimh, one of the Garvellach Islands, characteristic of Celtic religious practice. The islands of Iona and Lismore were centres for the production of illuminated manuscript copies of the Gospels, and Iona later housed a school of carvers of the low-relief grave-slabs characteristic of western Argyll. The oldest substantial evidence of Christianity in the area is the splendid Irish-style High Crosses of Kildalton (on Islay) and Iona; and there are also many simple early Christian cross-slabs, with good collections at Keills and Kilmory Knap, in Knapdale, both in the care of Historic Scotland. The influence of the Celtic Church persisted after Roman Catholicism became the 'official' religion in medieval Scotland in the eleventh century; and most of the surviving pre-Reformation church buildings in the area date from the period of Roman Catholic domination. The largest of these are the abbey church of Iona (c. 1200 on, **56**) and the much-altered remains of the cathedral of Lismore (late thirteenth and early fourteenth century, **64**). On Iona, there are also the remains of a nunnery. Of the smaller parish churches, none survives intact, but there are good examples at Kilmory Knap, Kildalton, Old Killean and old Craignish. Characteristic of these buildings are small east windows with wide internal window surrounds, also found in the chapel at Dunstaffnage Castle (thirteenth century, Fig. 1). There is medieval fabric in the Church of the Three Holy Brethren, Lochgoilhead (**42**), rebuilt in the eighteenth century, and in Kilfinan (**30**), rebuilt in 1759. The ruins of St Blane's Chapel on Bute, built from the twelfth century onward, are set in an oval graveyard which may date back to the sixth century. St Mahew's Roman Catholic Church (Fig. 2), Cardross, dates in part from the fifteenth century, but its present condition dates from the 1950s, when it was extensively restored.

There are no surviving early post-Reformation churches in Argyll, strongly suggesting that the medieval parish churches were adequate

Fig. 10. St Margaret's Roman Catholic Church, Lochgilphead, Argyll and Bute

for a stable population. When, as far as surviving church buildings suggest, building (and rebuilding) began in the second half of the eighteenth century, the earliest were largely vernacular in character. Kilcalmonell (c. 1760 and later, **28**), Dalavich (1770, **15**) and Kilchrenan (1770, **29**) are early examples, followed by South Knapdale (1775, **1**) and Jura (1776, **63**). The vernacular character of South Knapdale was later reduced by the addition of a tower. During the period when these small rural parish churches were being constructed, the first planned settlements were built. One of the first was Bowmore, on Islay; and, as the focal point, a splendid new church was built at the top of the main street to serve the village and its surrounding parish. Kilarrow (1767, **59**) is Scotland's only 'modern' round church. Though the plan was never replicated, the notion of a symmetrical 'set-piece' was influential. In 1783, Kilmodan (**34**) was built in Glendaruel, a typical vernacular T-plan church but with an advanced central bay surmounted by a pediment – a simple classical treatment which was copied (more or less) in a number of Argyll churches. The first, and probably the best, was Killean and Kilchenzie (1787–91, **31**), replacing a medieval church. It later gained a belfry, reducing the classical effect. Later examples of classical rural churches were Colonsay (1802, **54**), North Knapdale, Kilmichael of Inverlussa (1820, Fig. 3) and, last of all, Craignish (1826, **12**). To these should be added Glenaray and Inveraray (1792, **25**), the centrepiece of Inveraray planned town, with its classical treatment doubled, as the church has two classical frontages, serving what were two churches – one English, one Gaelic. The classical treatment is much more sophisticated than that of the rural churches, but the idea is the same. This grouping, to which could be added the former English church in Campbeltown (and in some respects the Highland Church there, 1807, **8**), is without parallel in Scotland. While these churches were being built, some much simpler ones were being constructed, including Kilninver (1793, **37**) and probably Kilmelford

Fig. 11. Corran Esplanade Church of Scotland, Oban, Argyll and Bute

Fig. 12. St Gildas Roman Catholic Church,
Rosneath, Argyll and Bute

(1785, **33**). The latter was, however, much altered in 1890, so its original character is not known. On Bute, the former Rothesay High Church (now the United Church of Bute, 1796, **52**) is a big box of a church (like North Knapdale and Craignish), designed to accommodate the growing population attracted by Rothesay's cotton-spinning mills. It has been much altered and recently extended. In the churchyard is St Mary's Chapel, the remains of the choir of the sixteenth-century predecessor of the present building, reroofed in 1997. It contains fine mural monuments.

By the time the fashion for classical churches had ended, the Gothic was coming into vogue. Glenorchy and Innishael (1810, **20**) is a very unusual early Gothic Revival building, on an octagonal plan, with a tower. Kilmorich (1816, **35**), similar in plan, is smaller and simpler, one of the prettiest churches in Argyll. Its impact is increased by its site on a knoll. This is another rural church. Much more advanced is Dunoon High (1816, **18**), an urban church in the newly fashionable 'Heritors' Gothic, built at a time when Dunoon had become easy to reach by steamboat and was becoming a marine resort. The last of the vernacular churches were built in the 1820s: Kilberry (1821, **27**) and Kilchoman, Islay (1825–7, Fig. 4). The latter, now derelict, is fashionable to the extent of having pointed windows.

During the construction of his Highland roads and bridges, Thomas Telford became aware that in many parts of the Highlands and Islands there were large parishes with scattered and growing populations, so that existing churches were inadequate. He persuaded the Westminster Parliament to sanction the creation of new parishes and to pay for basic churches and manses, which were built to standard designs by William Thomson. Among these were the Islay church of Portnahaven (1828, **62**), the parish church of Iona (1828, **57**), the now-ruined church of Oa, Islay, and the disused church of Ulva, a small island off Mull. Though not a

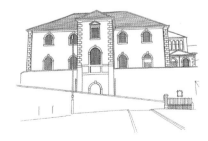

Fig. 13. The former Newark Parish Church,
Port Glasgow, Inverclyde

Parliamentary church, Muckairn (1829, **44**) has similar detailing. Kilmeny, Islay (1828, **58**) was remodelled at the same time as these churches, but is not of the standard design. The Telford/Thomson churches originally had long communion tables set across the buildings. Ardchattan (1836, Fig. 6) has a superb long table set along the building. It has 'Tudor' windows similar to those in the Parliamentary churches. Kilmartin (1835, **32**) is also in Tudor style, but is unusual in having side aisles.

On the Firth of Clyde and its linked sea lochs, the developing shoreline settlements needed churches. Little Ardentinny (1838–9, **4**) neat and simple, was one of the first. Colintraive (1840, **10**) is another, but jauntier. Garelochhead (Fig. 6) is similar; and the rather solemn Kilmun (1841, **36**), replacing a medieval building, a third. Innellan (1852, 1867, 1887, **24**) and Craigrownie (1853, 1869, **13**) had similar origins. Two early and large Free churches in Oban and Rothesay were also built to cope with steamboat-related expansion, as was the first church at Strone, whose tower survives (1858–9, **49**), though the body of the church was rebuilt in 1907–8.

The Disruption of 1843 that created the Free Church appears to have been welcomed warmly in the towns of Argyll and Bute. The Free High Church, Oban (1846) and Trinity, Rothesay (1845, **51**) were among the largest and finest first-generation Free churches in Scotland. There are small and early Free churches in Lochgilphead and in Minard, still in use as such. Later large Free churches in the area included Helensburgh West (1853, **22**), Cardross (1872, **9**) and St John's, Dunoon (1877, **19**). St John's was designed in part to accommodate the summer visitors to the resort. An unusual rural Free church is Kilcalmonell Free, Clachan (1878, Fig. 7). The United Presbyterian Church was formed in 1847 by amalgamating the United Secession Church and the Relief Church (both descendants of eighteenth-century breakaways from the Church of Scotland). It built large churches in Helensburgh (St Columba's, 1860, **23**) and in Campbeltown (Lorne and Lowland, 1872, **7**). A small United Presbyterian church in Cove later became a hall for Craigrownie (**13**).

In rural Argyll and Bute, however, the Free Church does not appear to have been particularly strong. The established Church of Scotland continued to build churches throughout the

Fig. 14. The former St Columba's Gaelic Chapel, Greenock, Inverclyde

Fig. 15. The former Union Street United
Secession Church, Greenock, Inverclyde
(demolished)

Victorian period. Some were small and simple, including Cumlodden near Furnace (1841, **14**), and Lochgair (1867, **40**). Others were more elaborate, such as St Modan's, Rosneath (1853, **48**), Ardrishaig (1860–8 and later, **5**), Kilbrandon, Seil (1866, **67**) and Luss (1875, **43**). The Rosneath and Luss churches were largely estate churches. All were Gothic Revival, and most have notable stained-glass windows.

From the 1880s until the First World War, the Church of Scotland built some very fine churches in Argyll. In Tarbert, a Scots Gothic church with a crown steeple was built on a striking site above the village (1886, **50**); and in Connel, St Oran's (1888, **11**) is a very pleasing essay in a different version of the Scots Gothic. Appin (1889, **2**), Tobermory (1895–6, Fig. 8) and Heylipol, Tiree (1902, **68**) are all more conventional, but St Kiaran's, Port Charlotte, Islay (1897, **60**) and Kilmore, Mull (1905, **66**) are in the Romanesque Revival style made popular by Peter Macgregor Chalmers of Glasgow. The design of St John's, Port Ellen (1897–8, **61**), also Romanesque, is – uniquely in Scotland – based on that of a church near Boulogne. The largest and perhaps the finest Romanesque church in Argyll and Bute is Kirn (1906–7, also Peter Macgregor Chalmers). The most unusual church of the period is St Conan's, Lochawe (**38**), the construction of which started in 1881–6 to designs by Walter Douglas Campbell, an amateur architect. It was enlarged in 1907 and not completed until 1930. It is an extraordinary assemblage of only marginally related features, but has a slightly surreal charm.

The other denomination which was active in church-building before 1914 was the Scottish Episcopal Church. Two of the earliest Episcopal churches in Argyll and Bute are Christ Church, Lochgilphead (1850–1, **41**) and St Columba's, Poltalloch (1852, **47**), both in mid-Argyll. St Columba's was built as an estate church. Later Episcopal churches include St Michael and All Angels,

Fig. 16. The former Gaelic Free Church, Greenock, Inverclyde

Fig. 17. Orangefield Baptist Church, Greenock, Inverclyde

Helensburgh (1868, 1930, **21**), All Saints, Inveraray (1885, **26**) and the little country church of St James, Ardbrecknish (1891, **3**). Construction of the first part of what is now St John's Episcopal Cathedral, Oban (**45**) began in 1863, though it did not reach its present form until 1968. Of the churches built by other denominations, perhaps the most interesting is Oban Congregational Church (1880, Fig. 9), the only late classical church in Argyll and Bute.

The formation of the United Free Church in 1900 by the amalgamation of the Free and United Presbyterian churches brought most of the Free churches in the area into the union, and thence into the Church of Scotland in 1929. The United Free had between 1900 and 1914 a programme of church extension. One of the rare examples in Argyll is Lochfyneside, Minard (1910, **39**), an iron church presumably built because the village's Free church did not join the union.

Since the First World War, few churches have been built in Argyll. The earliest is probably the island church on Gigha (1923–4, **55**), a simple Romanesque building. St Margaret's Roman Catholic Church, Lochgilphead (1927–9, Fig. 10) is also Romanesque, but a more accomplished design. A porch added in 1987 (not shown) has improved comfort but not the appearance. Between 1923 and 1931, a tall tower was added to All Saints Scottish Episcopal Church, Inveraray (**26**). In 1932, construction of St Columba's Roman Catholic Cathedral, Oban (**46**), was begun, though it was not completed until 1958. It is a dignified structure, built of Aberdeenshire granite, and replaced an iron church of 1886. At the other end of the scale, the little, very simple church of Kilchattan (**65**), on

Fig. 18. St Lawrence's Roman Catholic Church, Greenock, Inverclyde

Fig. 19. St Ninian's Parish Church, Larkfield, Greenock, Inverclyde

the island of Luing, was built as a mission church in 1936. After the Second World War, there was no need, as elsewhere in Scotland, to build large numbers of churches for expanding communities. The largest and finest church of the second half of the twentieth century is Corran Esplanade, Oban (1954–7, Fig. 11), an effective blend of traditional and modern. The modest church of St Peter and St Paul, Arrochar (1953) and the striking St Gildas, Rosneath (1968, Fig. 12) were both built for the Roman Catholic Church. Probably the most recent church in the area is the Church of Scotland's Dunbeg (1981, **16**), built to serve a new suburb of Oban. Cowal Baptist Church, Dunoon (**17**) was converted from an American servicemen's YMCA.

Finally, I will mention two extraordinary churches which were never places for public worship. The first is the private chapel of the Marquesses of Bute at Mount Stuart (1896–1903), with its stunning white marble interior. The second is the chapel of the Cardross Seminary of the Roman Catholic Church (1962–8). Acclaimed as a masterpiece of the Modern Movement, it had lost its function by 1979, and it is now empty and decaying.

Inverclyde

The fragmented land mass of Argyll is in stark contrast to the compact area of Inverclyde, dominated by the linear conurbation of Port Glasgow, Greenock and Gourock. Outside these, there are the large village of Kilmacolm and smaller settlements at Langbank, Inverkip and Wemyss Bay. The rest of the area (until 1975 part of the old county of Renfrewshire) is occupied by farmland and moorland. Originally squeezed into a narrow strip of ground along the coast of the Clyde estuary, Port Glasgow, Greenock and Gourock expanded after 1945 on to the higher ground to the south, and new churches were built in the two former to serve the suburbs thus created. From the late eighteenth century to the late twentieth century, Port Glasgow and Greenock were important industrial centres; and fluctuations in the fortunes of industry have had a significant impact on church provision.

The oldest surviving component of a church is the thirteenth-century aisle of Kilmacolm Old Church, also the only physical evidence of pre-

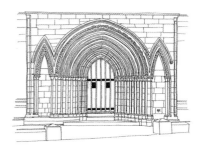

Fig. 20. West doorway, Paisley Abbey Church of Scotland, Renfrewshire

Reformation church-building in the area. After the Reformation, the first church to be built, in 1591, was at what was then the west end of Greenock. It was a small cruciform building, and survived on its original site until the 1920s, when the Belfast shipbuilders Harland and Wolff wished to expand Caird's shipbuilding yard, adjacent to the church. The congregation agreed to sell the building to the firm, which agreed to relocate the building to a site at the east end of the Esplanade. It was duly rebuilt in an approximation to its original form (1926–8, **74**); ironically, the yard extension was never completed. Port Glasgow was established by the merchants of Glasgow in the 1660s to handle their overseas trade, and both it and Greenock prospered as ports trading with the West Indian and North American colonies. Between 1759 and 1761, the citizens of Greenock built the Mid Kirk, a fine classical structure, which was given its steeple in 1787. It is now Wellpark Mid Kirk (**86**). The former Newark Church, Port Glasgow (1774, Fig. 13) is also evidence of a prosperous period that ended with the American War of Independence. The Shaw Stewarts of Ardgowan owned much of Greenock, and in 1804–5 they built a handsome new church at their estate village of Inverkip (**87**).

From the late eighteenth century, Greenock became an entry point for Gaelic-speaking migrants from the western Highlands and Islands wishing to improve their material conditions. Many emigrated to North America or made their way to the industries of Paisley and district and the Glasgow area. Some, however, settled in Greenock, and in 1823 a large new church – St Columba's Gaelic Chapel – was built to serve them (Fig. 14). This is classically detailed, as is St Andrew's Parish Church, Port Glasgow (**90**), built in the same year. Kilmacolm Old (1830, **88**) is the oldest surviving Gothic Revival church

Fig. 21. The former Castle Semple Collegiate Church, Lochwinnoch, Renfrewshire

in the area, followed soon after by Old Gourock and Ashton (1832, **73**). Greenock West United Reformed Church (1839-40, **85**) is also in that style, but with the flat frontage which, borrowed from the college chapels of Oxford and Cambridge, was especially suited to churches on restricted sites on urban streets. Interest in Greenock in the classical was not, however, exhausted. Union Street (now demolished, 1843-5, Fig. 15) was a 'flat classical' building, a style favoured by its builder, the United Secession Church. The building now known as Westburn Parish Church (**79**) is much grander. The body of the building was built in 1840 as a replacement for the Old West Church, but the steeple was not added until 1855, by which time it was stylistically outmoded, though very beautiful. The effects of the Disruption of 1843 were felt in Inverclyde, as in other urban centres. A Gaelic Free Church (1844, Fig. 16) was speedily built, and a large Free church was constructed in Gourock in 1857 (St John's, **72**). It acquired a tower with a crown steeple in 1878.

The migration of Highland and Irish Roman Catholics into Inverclyde created a demand for churches. Those of St John the Baptist, Port Glasgow (1854 and later, **93**), a 'college chapel' Gothic Revival building, and St Mary's, Greenock (1862, **80**), also Gothic, were the first, followed by St Ninian's, Gourock (1878 and later, **70**). The Scottish Episcopal Church built small churches in Gourock (St Bartholomew's, 1857, **71**) and Port Glasgow (St Mary the Virgin, 1857-8). The latter was demolished for road improvement and replaced by a new church in 1983-4 (**91**). The Episcopal Church also built a large church in Greenock in 1877-8 (St John the Evangelist, **78**) to replace a building of 1824-5. Among the Victorian buildings of smaller denominations are Baptist churches in Greenock (Orangefield, 1877, Fig. 17; and George Square, 1888) and in Gourock; Greenock Methodist Church (1883, **82**); and Port Glasgow United Reformed Church (**94**), built for the Evangelical Union.

The major Presbyterian denominations built several large churches in Greenock in the later nineteenth century. The United Presbyterians built what is now Ardgowan (**75**) in 1871. The Church

Fig. 22. St John's Parish Church, Lochwinnoch, Renfrewshire

Fig. 23. Holy Trinity Scottish Episcopal Church, Paisley, Renfrewshire

of Scotland constructed what is now Finnart St Paul's (**77**) in 1893 (replacing an iron church of 1878), and the Free Church built what was latterly St George's North (originally the Middle Free, recently closed) in 1870–1. The first two are Gothic, and the third is in a mixed Renaissance style with a tall steeple. The elaboration of these three buildings is evidence of the wealth of Greenock at the time. The last Gothic Revival churches to be built in Inverclyde were the elaborate St Columba's, Kilmacolm (1901–3, **89**) and the simple Mount Kirk, Greenock (1910, **84**). Both were constructed by the United Free Church, which had been formed in 1900 by the union of the Free and United Presbyterian Churches.

Inverclyde was badly affected by the trade depressions of the interwar period. Apart from the relocation of the Old West Church (see above), the only church built during that period was St Patrick's Roman Catholic Church, Greenock (1935, **76**), a daringly modern brick-faced building. The earlier Roman Catholic Church of St Lawrence, Cartsdyke, was destroyed in the Greenock blitz of 1941 and was replaced in 1954 by a striking new brick church (Fig. 18). By that time, the crowded slums of both Greenock and Port Glasgow were being replaced by new suburbs to the south and west, a process that continued into the 1970s. Both the Roman Catholic Church and the Church of Scotland built new Extension churches to serve these suburbs. Examples are St Ninian's Church of Scotland, Larkfield, Greenock (1952, Fig. 19) and St Francis's Roman Catholic Church, Port Glasgow (1974, **92**), both in simple modernist style. More unusual are the copper-roofed new St Mary the Virgin Scottish Episcopal Church, Port Glasgow (1983–4, **91**), in one of the new suburbs, and Greenock East United Reformed Church (1968, **83**), in a plain but striking style. The most

Fig. 24. Elderslie Parish Church, Renfrewshire

recent new church in the area is the Holy Rosary Chapel, Greenock (2004, **81**), built as part of the redevelopment of a convent.

Renfrewshire

This local-authority area, the central part of the pre-1975 county of the same name, contrasts markedly with Argyll and Bute and with Inverclyde. Much of it is flat, with river valleys penetrating the hinterland. Its eastern edge abuts Glasgow and what is now East Renfrewshire. Its only towns are Paisley and Johnstone, though they really form a single urban area, with Linwood and Elderslie between them, and Renfrew to the north of Paisley. Despite their proximity to Glasgow and to each other, all these places retain distinctive characters and strong senses of local pride. Other places of interest are the villages of Kilbarchan, Lochwinnoch, Houston and Bridge of Weir, all former textile settlements. The new town of Erskine was established in the early 1970s, but has never really established itself as a place. Linwood was expanded to serve a new car factory, but has suffered hardship since the plant closed in 1981.

Paisley is the only major town in the area, and has been its natural centre since the twelfth century, when its Cluniac abbey was founded by Walter Fitz Alan, High Steward to David I. The abbey became powerful and prosperous, and a significant part of the abbey church survived the Reformation, when the nave was retained as the parish church of the town, and the south transept was used as a family chapel. The tower collapsed in 1553, taking with it the crossing, the north transept and the choir. These parts were reinstated in the late nineteenth and early twentieth century – though, as little contemporary evidence survived, the reconstruction was largely conjectural (**102**, Fig. 20). The only other significant pre-Reformation church in the area is Castle Semple Collegiate Church, Lochwinnoch, roofless but otherwise complete (1504–5, Fig. 21). It is now in the care of Historic Scotland.

In the early eighteenth century, the area began to be noted for its textile trade, with Paisley at its centre. Kilbarchan became a centre for handloom weaving at that time, and a new church was built in 1724. Much of this building survives, rebuilt as a hall for Kilbarchan West Church

Fig. 25. St Fillan's Roman Catholic Church, Houston, Renfrewshire

Fig. 26. St Matthew's Church of the Nazarene,
Paisley, Renfrewshire

(1899–1901, **99**). At Lochwinnoch, the west end of St Winoc's Church (probably early eighteenth century) has been retained as a clock-tower. The Laigh Church, Paisley (1736–8), now an arts centre, was one of the largest early eighteenth-century churches in Scotland. As the town expanded to the west, the High Church (now Oakshaw Trinity, 1756, **112**) was built. This is one of a series of large burgh churches built in growing West of Scotland communities in the mid-eighteenth century. Its steeple was added in 1770, to a somewhat outmoded design. Other large eighteenth-century churches were built by the Secessions: Castlehead, Paisley (1781 and later, **104**) and Kilbarchan East (1789, **100**). By that time, Johnstone had been founded as a planned town (1782) and had opened its first cotton-spinning mill in the same year. Johnstone High Church was opened in 1792 (**98**), a late example of an octagonal church. The last in Scotland was St John's Parish, Lochwinnoch (1806, Fig. 22), built to serve the replanned weaving village. In 1793, a simple Gaelic chapel was built in Oakshaw to serve migrants from the Highlands and Islands. A classical Methodist church was built in Paisley in 1810, probably to serve English migrants. It is now the Church of the New Jerusalem (**109**), the last Swedenborgian church in Scotland. Also from 1810 is the former Cameronian (Reformed Presbyterian) Church in Oakshaw, now flats, as is the former St George's Church of Scotland, George Street (1819), built to replace the Laigh Church. The flat classical former Oakshaw East Church of Scotland was built in 1826 as a United Secession church, similar to the Union Church in Greenock (see Fig. 15). Holy Trinity Scottish Episcopal Church, Paisley (1828 and 1884, Fig. 23) appears to have been the first church in the area for that denomination. This is a very plain simple Gothic building, as are two other Paisley churches, built to serve new suburbs: the former Martyrs' Church, Woodside Cemetery, now a hall (1835); and St Luke's, Neilston Road (1836). Other churches built to serve

Fig. 27. St Mary's Scottish Episcopal Church,
Bridge of Weir, Renfrewshire

Fig. 28. Methodist Central Halls, Paisley, Renfrewshire

textile communities are Elderslie (1840, Fig. 24) and the Roman Catholic Church of St Fillan, Houston (1841, Fig. 25).

The Disruption of 1843 was quickly followed by the construction of the first Free churches in Paisley. The former Orr Square Church of Scotland was built as the Free High (1845), speedily followed by Martyrs' (1847, 1904–5, **108**). Later Free churches included St John's, Oakshaw (1862–3), and Sherwood in the east end of the town (1891–2; spire of 1927 has been removed).

The town of Paisley was dominated from the later nineteenth century until the 1970s by the cotton-thread-making mills of the Coats and Clark families (Ferguslie and Anchor mills). The Clark family paid for much of the reconstruction of the abbey church, while the Coats family underpinned the construction of St James's United Presbyterian Church (1880–4, **105**), a very grand Gothic Revival building. After the union in 1900 of the United Presbyterian and Free Churches as the United Free Church, they paid for Wallneuk (now Wallneuk North) Church (1915, **107**), a superb late Gothic building. A slightly earlier United Free church is the former St George's United Free Church (now St Matthew's Church of the Nazarene, 1905–7, Fig. 26), a very important Art Nouveau building. St Mary's Roman Catholic Church (1891, **110**) is a typical Pugin & Pugin building of a type commoner in Glasgow and Lanarkshire. Perhaps the most remarkable Paisley church is the Thomas Coats Memorial Baptist Church (1894, **106**), built by the Coats family as a tribute to Thomas, who ran the Ferguslie Mills for many years and who was a notable Baptist. The building is more like a cathedral than a Baptist church, but a superb piece of late Gothic Revival design.

While these Paisley churches were being constructed, other parts of the area were building new churches, mostly in Gothic Revival style. The finest is probably Renfrew Old (1862, **116**), on an ancient site, and containing a medieval altar-tomb and a tomb of 1633 from an earlier building on

Fig. 29. The former Roman Catholic Church of Our Holy Redeemer, Elderslie, Renfrewshire (demolished)

Fig. 30. St Bernadette's Roman Catholic Church, Erskine, Renfrewshire

the site. Others include Houston and Killellan (1874, **96**), effectively an estate church, and St Machar's, Ranfurly (1878, **115**), built to serve a textile village being transformed into an upper middle-class commuter settlement, as was St Mary's Scottish Episcopal Church, Bridge of Weir, a simple Arts and Crafts building (1909, Fig. 27). Kilbarchan West (1899–1901, **99**) is a late example of the Gothic Revival, replacing an earlier church (1724; see earlier). The Methodist Central Halls, Paisley (1908, Fig. 28), in Edwardian Baroque style, look more like a commercial building than a church.

There were few churches built in Renfrewshire between the wars. The largest was St Mirin's Roman Catholic Church, Paisley (1931, **103**), a simple Romanesque building. It became the cathedral church for the Diocese of Paisley when it was carved out of the Archdiocese of Glasgow in 1947. The creation of new suburbs to house people displaced by slum clearance from the centre of the town led to the building of new churches by the Roman Catholic Church and the Church of Scotland. Among the Roman Catholic churches are or were St Peter's, Glenburn (1958, **111**), Our Holy Redeemer, Elderslie (1971, Fig. 29) and St Charles's, Charleston (1986, **113**). Our Holy Redeemer was closed in 2003 and has been demolished. The construction of Erskine New Town led to the building of two Roman Catholic churches, St John Bosco's (1979) and St Bernadette's (1983, Fig. 30). The Church of Scotland built Erskine New (1977, Fig. 31). All these postwar buildings, and others not mentioned, were built economically but imaginatively. So, too, were new Church of Scotland buildings at Linwood (1965, **101**) and Inchinnan (1968, **97**). Linwood is appropriately industrial in character. Inchinnan replaced a church demolished during the development of Glasgow Airport. It originally had a flat roof, but this has been replaced by a pitched roof. In the grounds of this building is a noted, though small, collection of early Christian carved stones, linking this church to the earliest physical evidence of Christianity in Renfrewshire. The Barochan Cross, now in Paisley Abbey Church, is in a similar style.

West Dunbartonshire

The old county of Dunbartonshire was in two distinct parts, separated by Glasgow and part of Stirlingshire. The western part, traditionally known as

Fig. 31. Erskine Parish Church, Renfrewshire

Lennox, became a separate local-authority area in 1975, but a large part of its western edge was split off in 1996 and joined to Argyll and Bute, which, indeed, it resembles in character. The present council area consists of the largely urbanised north bank of the Clyde from Yoker to Dumbarton, the Vale of Leven from Dumbarton to Balloch, and a tract of rural country to the south-east of Loch Lomond. Dumbarton and Clydebank are the largest settlements, with a string of industrial places along the River Leven: Renton, Alexandria, Bonhill and Balloch. In the rural area are Gartocharn and Kilmaronock. Dumbarton was from the eighteenth century a centre of shipbuilding, joined in the later nineteenth century by Clydebank and Dalmuir. The Clydebank shipyard of John Brown & Co. built what were until recently the largest passenger ships in the world, the RMS *Queen Mary* and *Queen Elizabeth*, while the celebrated tea clipper *Cutty Sark* was built in Dumbarton. Along the Vale of Leven, there were from the eighteenth century until the early twentieth century a string of bleachworks, dyeworks and calico-printing works which served world markets. The other major industry of the area was from the 1880s to the 1970s the making of sewing machines at the Singer Works at Kilbowie, part of Clydebank. This was for many years the largest sewing-machine works in the world.

At Dumbarton there is a volcanic plug, the site of Dumbarton Castle, but in the first millennium AD the centre of the British (Brythonic Celtic) kingdom of Strathclyde. It is likely that, though primarily a centre of secular power, Dumbarton Rock had a sacred meaning for the kingdom. Medieval Christianity is now only represented by an arch of the fifteenth-century Collegiate Chapel of the Blessed Virgin Mary in Dumbarton, re-erected in the grounds of the Municipal

Fig. 32. Old Kilpatrick Parish Church, West Dunbartonshire

Fig. 33. Duntocher West United Free Church
(ex-United Secession), Clydebank,
West Dunbartonshire

Buildings in 1907. The oldest church in the area is now Riverside Parish Church, Dumbarton (1811, **123**), a plain church with a fine classical steeple. It replaced a church built in 1565, only five years after the Reformation. Its graveyard contains the burial place of the Napier family, inextricably linked to the development of the steamship. In the following year, a very different church was built in Old Kilpatrick, one of the first 'Heritors' Gothic buildings, rectangular, with a pinnacled tower on one end (1812, Fig. 32). Bonhill Parish Church (1836) is also an essay in that style. In 1813, the delightful Georgian rural church of Kilmaronock (**122**) was opened, with large small-paned windows giving it a unique elegance. This contrasts markedly with the severe simplicity of two former United Secession churches: Duntocher West United Free (1822, Fig. 33), and Vale of Leven Baptist, Alexandria (1843, Fig. 34). The former St Andrew's Parish Church, Alexandria, with its unusual steeple, dates from 1840. Three years later, the Disruption took place, forming the Free Church – and one of the first churches of the new denomination in the area was in Renton, where the Millburn Free Church was built between 1843 and 1845 (Fig. 35). It is a miniature version of the contemporary St John's Free Church, Glasgow, and is alas derelict. The first Free church in Dumbarton was built in 1844 and rebuilt in 1877, but is now demolished. The Gothic Revival High Free (1864), with a notable steeple, survives in secular use. There is a large former United Presbyterian church at West Bridgend, Dalreoch (1887–8), also in Gothic Revival style, with a wheel window in the gable, characteristic of many United Presbyterian churches. St Augustine's Scottish Episcopal Church (1873, **124**) is a handsome feature of the High Street, but never received its intended steeple. St Patrick's Roman Catholic Church (1903, **121**) replaced an earlier church of the same name, built in 1830. A detached tower was added in 1925–6. After the Second World War, two new Roman Catholic churches were built. The more interesting

Fig. 34. Vale of Leven Baptist Church
(ex-United Secession), Alexandria,
West Dunbartonshire

Fig. 35. The former Millburn Free Church, Renton, West Dunbartonshire

is St Michael's, Dalreoch (1954), with diamond-shaped windows.

Up the Vale of Leven, the pinnacled red sandstone Renton Trinity Church was built as the parish church (1892, **125**). St Martin of Tours Roman Catholic Church (1970) is an unusual modernist building next to the former Millburn Free (see Fig. 35). Alexandria has a Scottish Episcopal church, St Mungo's (1894, **117**), with an uncompleted south aisle; its Church of Scotland parish church is now in a postwar housing area (1965, **118**), in a character appropriate to its setting. It also serves Balloch, which has a small, neat Roman Catholic church, St Kessog's (1958). On the east side of the Leven is Jamestown, once a flourishing calico-printing village, now much reduced. Its parish church (1869–70), with a tall steeple, survives.

Clydebank's churches suffered badly during the air raids of 1941, as did the housing which took the brunt of these attacks. In the postwar period, as elsewhere in the West of Scotland, new housing estates grew up round the old town centre, linking Clydebank to the once-separate community of Duntocher. The Roman Catholic Church of Our Holy Redeemer in 'old Clydebank' (1903), of the West of Scotland Pugin & Pugin type, survived the blitz, as did Kilbowie St Andrew's Church of Scotland (1904, with a tower of 1933, **119**). The only Church of Scotland building in the town centre is Abbotsford, almost industrial in character. To the north is St Eunan's Roman Catholic Church (1951), severely functional but with a fine interior.

The same architects, Gillespie, Kidd & Coia, designed St Joseph's Roman Catholic Church, Faifley (1963–4), but this was destroyed by fire in the mid-1990s. It has been replaced by a fine new church (1997, **120**). Faifley Church of Scotland (Fig. 36) was constructed in 1956. New churches were also

Fig. 36. Faifley Parish Church, Clydebank, West Dunbartonshire

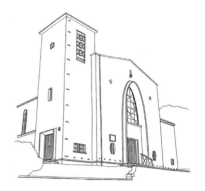

Fig. 37. Duntocher Trinity Parish Church, Clydebank, West Dunbartonshire

built in Duntocher. The Church of Scotland, Duntocher Trinity (1950–2, Fig. 37), is a striking brick-faced building built with government compensation for the destruction in the blitz of the previous church on the site. A new Roman Catholic church, St Mary's (1954), also replaced an earlier building. In Radnor Park, west of the town centre, its Congregational church replaced a blitz-damaged predecessor, and in 1978–80 a striking Methodist church was constructed in 'brutalist' style. Dalmuir, to the west of Clydebank, has a postwar Roman Catholic church (St Stephen's, 1958) and a Church of Scotland, Dalmuir Barclay, built a few years ago to replace an earlier building destroyed by fire. The most unusual modern church in Clydebank is St Margaret's Roman Catholic Church (Gillespie, Kidd & Coia, 1972), a low brick building hidden behind earth banks, and with a 'space-frame' flat roof.

Conclusion

The churches of Argyll and Clyde are, as can be seen, as varied as any in the whole of Scotland. The area can claim to be the cradle of modern Christianity in Scotland – and its legacy of small chapels in remote areas, and of great urban churches, reminds us of the power of the spiritual over many centuries. There are many opportunities to savour the extraordinary diversity of approaches to worship in the area, and to contemplate the different architectural styles thought appropriate to those approaches. Open your mind to difference, be challenged, and be stimulated by the stripped buildings and theology of some denominations, and by the richly ritual and visual approach of others. And, perhaps most movingly of all, seek out some of the places which can trace their Christian roots to the early Celtic missionaries. On the way, you will see some of the finest scenery in all of Scotland, and in visiting urban areas gain a feeling for what modern Scotland is really like. Go and see, with open eyes and loving hearts. You will not be disappointed.

Professor John R. Hume
Universities of Glasgow and St Andrews

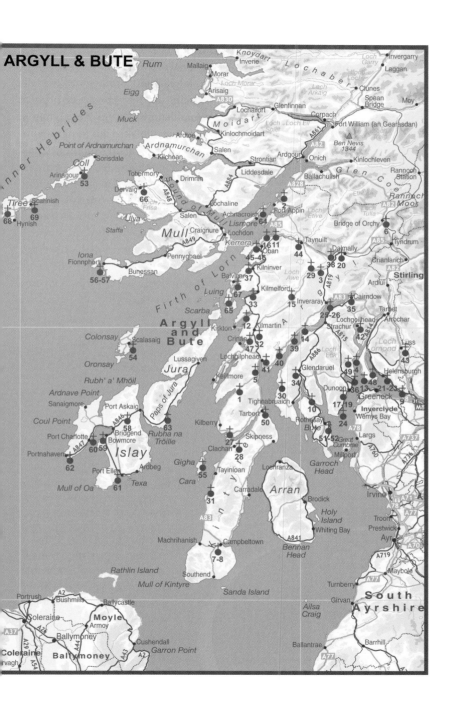

ARGYLL & BUTE

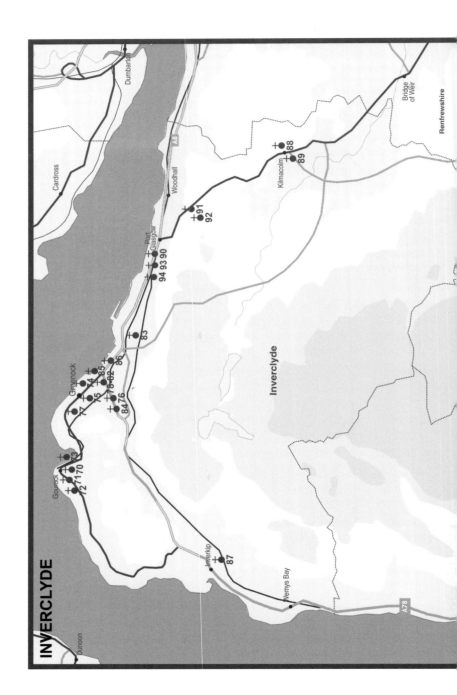

INVERCLYDE

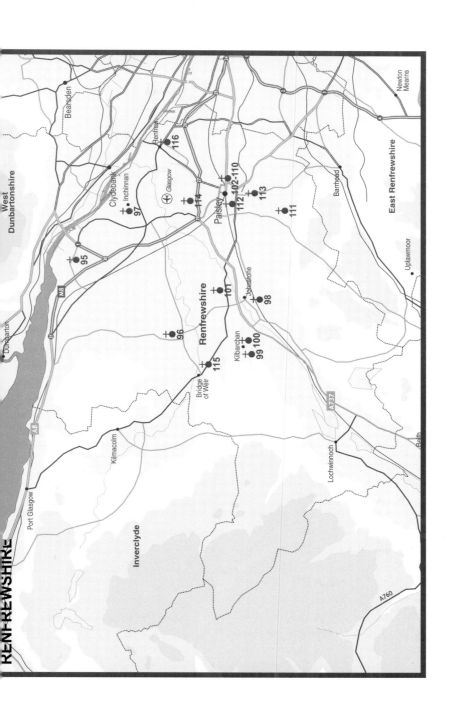

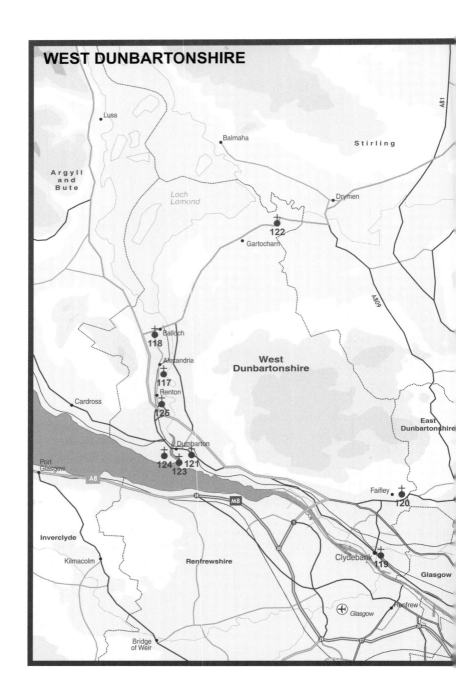

WEST DUNBARTONSHIRE

Luss

Balmaha

Stirling

Argyll
and
Bute

Loch
Lomond

Drymen

122

Gartocharn

A809

Balloch
118

West
Dunbartonshire

Alexandria

117

Renton

Cardross

125

East
Dunbartonshire

Dumbarton

Port
Glasgow

124 **121**
123

Faifley

120

A8

M8

Inverclyde

Clydebank

119

Glasgow

Kilmacolm

Renfrewshire

Glasgow

Renfrew

Bridge
of Weir

How to use this Guide

Entries are arranged by local-authority area, with large areas sub-divided for convenience. The number preceding each entry refers to the map. Each entry is followed by symbols for access and facilities:

⅄	Ordnance Survey reference	✺	Hearing induction loop for the deaf
🏠	Denomination	👤	Welcomers and guides on duty
⊕	Church website	📖	Guidebooks and souvenirs available/for sale
•	Regular services		
○	Church events	NADFAS	Church Recorders' Inventory (NADFAS)
•	Opening arrangements		
♿	Wheelchair access for partially abled	☕	Refreshments
WC	Toilets available for visitors	Ⓐ	Category A listing
		Ⓑ	Category B listing
WC	Toilets adapted for the disabled available for visitors	Ⓒ	Category C listing

Category A: Buildings of national or international importance, either architectural or historic, or fine little-altered examples of some particular period, style or building type.

Category B: Buildings of regional or more than local importance, or major examples of some particular period, style or building type which may have been altered.

Category C: Buildings of local importance, lesser examples of any period, style, or building type, as originally constructed or moderately altered; and simple traditional buildings which group well with others in categories A and B.

The information appearing in the gazetteer of this guide is supplied by the participating churches. While this is believed to be correct at the time of going to press, Scotland's Churches Scheme cannot accept any responsibility for its accuracy.

1 SOUTH KNAPDALE PARISH CHURCH, ACHAHOISH

**Achahoish
PA31 8PD**

NR 781 775

Church of Scotland

Linked with Ardrishaig (5)

B8024, 16km (10 miles) south-west of Lochgilphead

The parish of South Knapdale was formed in 1734, and churches were built at Achahoish and Inverneill (now a ruin). Achahoish was completed in 1775, rectangular in plan, with a square castellated tower added in the 19th century. Ancient font basin from St Columba's Cave.

- Sunday: 9.45am April to September, 12.30pm October to March
- Open daily (01546 603269)

2 APPIN PARISH CHURCH

**Appin
PA38 4BN**

NM 939 459

Church of Scotland

On A828, 19km (12 miles) south of Ballachulish

Granite Gothic Revival church of 1889, designed by Donald Macintyre. Two memorials for those who died in the First and Second World Wars. Millennium embroidery executed by the ladies of the village depicting life in Appin through the 20th century.

- Sunday: 10.00am
- Open 10.00am–4.00pm Monday to Saturday in June, July and August; or by arrangement (01631 730289)

❸ ST JAMES'S CHURCH, ARDBRECKNISH

**Ardbrecknish
Portsonachan
PA33 1BH**

🏔 NN 072 212

⛪ Scottish Episcopal

🌐 www.argyllandtheisles.org.uk/
ardbrecknish.html

Linked with St John's Cathedral, Oban (45)

On B840, 3km (2 miles) from junction with A819 at Cladich

St James's was built as a private chapel for the Thorpe family in 1891. Charming stone-built nave-and-chancel church with a stone interior with a fine series of monuments and excellent windows. Bells rehung 1991. Grass churchyard overlooking Loch Awe.

- Sunday: 11.00am in summer; 3.00pm on 3rd Sunday of the month in winter
- Open daylight hours in summer (01631 562323)

❹ ARDENTINNY CHURCH

**Shore Road
Ardentinny
PA23 8TR**

🏔 NS 188 876

⛪ Church of Scotland

🌐 www.cowalshorechurches.org.uk

Linked with Kilmun (36), Strone (49)

On Loch Long, 8km (5 miles) north of Strone

Simple oblong kirk of 1838–9 with three tall windows each side. Gabled front with gabled porch and arched bellcote at apex. Pulpit with sounding board decorated with finials. The church contains the memorials to the men of HMS *Armadillo*, the wartime Royal Navy commando unit who trained in Ardentinny.

- Sunday: 2.30pm
- Open daily (01369 840313)

5 ARDRISHAIG PARISH CHURCH

**Tarbert Road
Ardrishaig
PA30 8EP**

⚑ NR 854 852

🏛 Church of Scotland

Linked with South Knapdale (1)

On A83, 3km (2 miles) south of Lochgilphead

Gothic tower-fronted nave church of 1860 with low semi-octagonal transepts and vestibule added 1904. The octagonal castellated stage of the tower and the sharp spire were added in 1868. Edwardian Art Nouveau patterned stained glass in all windows.

- Sunday: 11.00am
- Open usually daily or by arrangement (01546 603269)

6 BRIDGE OF ORCHY PARISH CHURCH

Strathfillan Parish

**Bridge of Orchy
PA36 4AD**

⚑ NN 297 396

🏛 Church of Scotland

🌐 www.strathfillanparish.org.uk

Linked with Glenorchy (20), Crianlarich (Stirlingshire)

A82, next to Bridge of Orchy Hotel

Small whitewashed building with grey slate roof and red-painted gutters and downpipes, Bridge of Orchy Church looks just like a cottage. The church is set amid dramatic landscape and is a popular stop on the West Highland Way.

- 11.30am on 2nd and 4th Sunday of the month
- Open by arrangement (01838 200207)

7 LORNE & LOWLAND CHURCH, CAMPBELTOWN

The Longrow Church

**Longrow
Campbeltown
PA28 6ER**

NR 718 206

Church of Scotland

Built in 1872 to the design of John
Burnet, historically called the
Longrow Church. Classical, influenced
by Italian Renaissance style. Its bell-
tower is a well-known landmark. Two
stairways lead from the entrance
foyer to a horseshoe gallery. Fine
plaster ceiling. Pulpit integral with
organ case, 1895. Organ by Brindley &
Foster. Stained glass by W. & J. J. Keir.

- Sunday: 11.15am
- Open July to August, Monday to
  Friday 11.00am–4.00pm; at other
  times by arrangement (01586
  552612)

8 HIGHLAND PARISH CHURCH, CAMPBELTOWN

The Old Kirk

**New Quay Street
Campbeltown
PA28 6BA**

NR 720 201

Church of Scotland

www.highlandparishchurch.org.
uk

'To be causewayed with whinstone
and paved with hewn flags. The lock
on the front door to be of 20/- value
and the rest to have snecks and
wooden bolts': the instruction of
the architect George Dempster of
Greenock, for a new church, built
for the Highland, Gaelic-speaking,
congregation of the area, and
completed in 1807. The planned belfry
was not large enough for the heritors,
so a steeple was built; it has been
rebuilt twice since, the casualty of
lightning strikes. Allen Renaissance
organ, 2000. The organ screen bears a
memorial to the fallen of the Second
World War.

- Sunday: 11.15am and 6.30pm, except
  July and August
- Open daily

9 CARDROSS PARISH CHURCH

**Station Road
Cardross
G82 5NL**

NS 345 775

Church of Scotland

On A814

A church was founded in 1225 on the west bank of the River Leven and rebuilt in the village in 1640. The present building of 1872, by John Burnet, with nave and tower, was originally built for the Free Church. Stained-glass windows by Sadie McLellan, 1972, embroidered panels by Hannah Frew Paterson, 1981, woven silk hangings by Sarah Sumsion, 1990, and engraved glass windows by John Lawrie, 1992. Peal of eight bells.

- Sunday: 9.30am and 11.00am; June, July and August 10.00am only
- Open Monday, Wednesday, Thursday and Friday mornings, or by arrangement (01389 841509)

10 COLINTRAIVE CHURCH

West Cowal Parish

**Kyles View
Colintraive
PA22 3AS**

NS 045 735

Church of Scotland

Linked with Kilfinan (30), Kilmodan (34)

On the Kyles of Bute, 1.6km (1 mile) south of ferry to Bute

Erected 1840 by Mrs Campbell of Southhall as a chapel of ease, part of Inverchaolain parish. Became a Free Church in 1843, then United Free in 1900, and returned to the Church of Scotland in 1929. Spectacular views over Kyles of Bute.

- Sunday: 10.00am or 11.30am, alternating monthly with Kilmodan
- Open daily (01369 820232)

11 ST ORAN'S CHURCH, CONNEL

Connel
PA37 1PJ

⚲ NM 914 343
⛪ Church of Scotland
🌐 www.connelchurch.co.uk

Linked with Dunbeg (16), Coll (53)

On A85

Gothic Revival cruciform church of 1888 with lancet and pointed traceried windows, gabled porch and a central tower with corbelled parapet. Good interior with open timbered ceiling and stone arches supporting the tower at the crossing. Fine collection of 20th-century glass by various artists. Beautiful views up Loch Etive from garden.

• Sunday: 10.30am
• Open daily (01631 710242)

12 CRAIGNISH PARISH CHURCH

Ardfern
PA31 8QN

⚲ NM 805 042
⛪ Church of Scotland

Linked with Kilmelford (33), Kilninver (37), Kilchattan, Luing (65), Kilbrandon, Seil (67)

South side of Ardfern village on B8002

Attractive Georgian-style building of 1826 with hipped roof and harled masonry walls. Simple rectangular plan with vestry to rear, front façade dominated by a pediment and short tower. Lancet windows have fine fenestration. Symmetry in front and side elevations maintained by trompe-l'oeil windows. Inside, a fine tiered precentor's box and pulpit.

• Sunday: 10.00am
• Open daily (01852 500277)

13 CRAIGROWNIE CHURCH

**Church Road
Cove
G84 0LZ**

NS 224 810

Church of Scotland

Linked with St Modan's, Rosneath (48)

At Barons Point, between Kilcreggan and Cove

Daughter church of Rosneath, opened 1853. Low Arts & Crafts church by David Cousin, enlarged by Honeyman & Keppie, 1889. Organ by James J. Binns of Leeds. Various examples of stained glass including J. Benson, S. Adam, Mayer & Co. Frescoes of the four Evangelists by the sisters Doris and Anna Zinkeisen. Nearby church hall in a former church designed by Hugh Barclay, 1858, with windows by F. Hase-Hayden, A. Webster, A. McW. Webster and others.

- Sunday: 10.00am in even-numbered years, 11.30am in odd-numbered years
- Open by arrangement (01436 842254)

     (by arrangement)

14 CUMLODDEN PARISH CHURCH

**Furnace
PA32 8XU**

NS 015 997

Church of Scotland

Linked with Lochfyneside (39), Lochgair (40)

On A83, 1.6km (1 mile) south-west of Furnace

Simple stone church with slate roof, built in 1841 by local mason David Crow to a design by James Nairn of Balloch. Interior redesigned 1894. Contains an early Christian cross-shaft showing a bearded figure, 8th or 9th century, removed from Killevin burial ground. Stained glass 1924 by William Meikle & Sons, Glasgow.

- Sunday: 10.30am
- Open by arrangement (01499 500288)

Gaelic

15 DALAVICH CHURCH

**Dalavich
PA35 1HL**

A NM 968 124

Church of Scotland

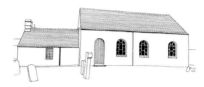

Linked with Kilchrenan (29), Muckairn (44)

North shore road of Loch Awe

The building dates from about 1770 in a traditional style. Small, simple but dignified oblong with whitewashed walls and round-headed windows. The church sits in a burial enclosure close to the shore of Loch Awe. A small bell-tower was built on the gable to celebrate the Millennium.

- Sunday: 10.00am, 2nd and 4th Sunday of the month
- Open by arrangement (01866 822677)

16 DUNBEG PARISH CHURCH

**Etive Road
Dunbeg
PA37 1QF**

A NM 878 334

Church of Scotland

www.connelchurch.co.uk/

Linked with Connel (11), Coll (53)

Off A85, second left

The church in Dunbeg started as a Nissen hut in the early 1940s, when the Admiralty built prefabs to house dock workers and the village was born. The present church was built in 1981 to replace the Nissen hut. It is a simple hall-church with low eaves and a large window in the apex of the gable.

- Sunday: 12.00 noon
- Open by arrangement (01631 710242)

17 COWAL BAPTIST CHURCH, DUNOON

**Alfred Street
Dunoon
PA23 8AB**

⚐ NS 172 771
⛪ Baptist
🌐 www.cowalbaptistchurch.org

Cowal Baptist Church meets for Sunday worship in the Senior Citizens Club premises in Alfred Street, Dunoon, which, at some time in the past, was a Congregational church.

- Sunday: 11.00am and 6.30pm
- Open Monday to Saturday 10.00am–4.00pm (01369 704520)

18 DUNOON HIGH KIRK

**Church Square
Dunoon
PA23 7DN**

⚐ NS 173 769
⛪ Church of Scotland
🌐 www.dunoon-highkirk.org.uk

Linked with Innellan (24)

The present building probably stands on the site of a much earlier church which until 1688 was the Cathedral Church of both the Roman Catholic and Episcopalian Bishops of Argyll. Stone from this early church was used to build Gillespie Graham's Late Decorated Gothic Revival church of 1816. The belfry tower was added in 1839, and the church was lengthened and widened by Andrew Balfour in 1909. Chancel window 1939 by Douglas Hamilton. Gravestones of the 13th and 17th centuries in the kirkyard.

- Sunday: 11.00am; midweek service Wednesday: 10.30am
- Open Monday to Saturday 10.30am–4.00pm; other times by arrangement (01369 702858)

19 ST JOHN'S CHURCH, DUNOON

**Argyll Street
Dunoon
PA23 7AB**

ᛉ NS 172 769

🏛 Church of Scotland

A magnificent nave-and-aisles kirk by R. A. Bryden of 1877, built to supersede the original Free Church on the same site. Normandy Gothic-style spired tower and galleried 'concert hall' interior. Raised choir behind central pulpit. 3-manual pipe organ by Brook & Co., 1895. Interesting stained glass, including windows by Stephen Adam and Gordon Webster; also Lauder Memorial.

- Sunday: 10.15am; 6.30pm on last Sunday of the month
- Open June to September, Monday to Friday 10.00am–12.00 noon (01369 830639)

20 GLENORCHY & INNISHAEL PARISH CHURCH

Glenorchy Kirk

**Dalmally
PA33 1AS**

ᛉ NN 168 275

🏛 Church of Scotland

🌐 www.glenorchyparish.org.uk

Linked with Bridge of Orchy (6), Crianlarich (Stirlingshire)

On A85, near the head of Loch Awe

Octagonal Gothic church with square tower by James Elliot, 1810. Under the entrance to the church, 26 clan chiefs of the Macgregors lie buried. Fine stained-glass window of 1898. Major restoration, 1988–91. Burial ground has 14th- and 15th-century grave-slabs with interlaced floral designs. Tower restored, 2007–10.

- Sunday: 10.00am
- Open daily (01838 200207)

21 ST MICHAEL AND ALL ANGELS, HELENSBURGH

William Street Helensburgh G84 8BD

- NS 292 825
- Scottish Episcopal
- www.stmichaelhelensburgh.org. uk

Off Clyde Street

Built by Robert Rowand Anderson in 1868 in French Gothic style. Tower with peal of eight bells added in 1930. Richly decorated interior with oak chancel screen and elaborately carved Austrian oak north porch screen. West porch screen, 1996, of light oak and engraved glass by James Anderson. Alabaster and mosaic reredos against encaustic tiling. Organ originally by August Gern. Good stained glass by Clayton & Bell, Shrigley & Hunt, Adam & Small, and Barraud & Westlake, with five windows by C. E. Kempe including fine rose window in west façade.

- Sunday: 8.00am, 9.30am, 10.15am and 6.30pm; Tuesday: 10.30am; Wednesday: 7.30pm (check website for summer worship)
- Open daily 9.00am–5.00pm (01436 672500)

22 WEST KIRK OF HELENSBURGH

Colquhoun Square Helensburgh G84 8UP

- NS 295 825
- Church of Scotland
- www.westkirkofhelensburgh.com

Victorian Gothic building of 1853, W. H. & J. M. Hay, restored by Robert Wemyss after disastrous fire in 1924, with a porch by William Leiper. Impressive panelled interior, with fine woodwork and half-timbered ceiling. Organ by Hill, 1894, rebuilt by Hill, Norman & Beard. Exceptionally fine stained glass, including memorial windows to Andrew Bonar Law, one-time prime minister, and to John Logie Baird, inventor of television and son of the manse in Helensburgh.

- Sunday: 10.00am May to August, 11.00am September to April
- Open daily all year 9.00am–5.00pm (01436 676880)

23 ST COLUMBA'S, HELENSBURGH

**79–81 Sinclair Street
Helensburgh
G84 8TR**

NS 297 825

Church of Scotland

www.stcolumbahelensburgh.org

The King Street building, now the hall, was erected in 1845 as the United Secession Church. Margaret Bell, wife of Henry Bell (of steamship fame, and first provost of Helensburgh), was a founder member. The present church on Sinclair Street was built in 1860, architect William Spence (who probably also designed the hall). A tall square tower is the particular exterior feature; the interior is spacious with a horseshoe gallery. Organ by Harrison & Harrison.

- Sunday: 9.45am (informal in hall), 11.00am (traditional in main sanctuary)
- Open Saturday mornings June to August (ask at coffee morning in hall), or by arrangement (01436 675340)

24 INNELLAN PARISH CHURCH

**7 Matheson Lane
Innellan
PA23 7TA**

NS 152 707

Church of Scotland

Linked with Dunoon High (18)

Church of nave and aisles, built of local whin rubble in 1852 and expanded in 1867 and again in 1887. Fine stone pulpit of 1887. The central stained-glass window is a version of Holman Hunt's 'The Light of the World', which glows whatever the lighting conditions. The church is best known for its association with George Matheson, who ministered for 18 years from 1869, during which time he wrote 'O Love that wilt not let me go'.

- Sunday: 11.30am
- Open by arrangement

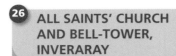

25 GLENARAY & INVERARAY PARISH CHURCH, INVERARAY

**Church Square
Inveraray
PA32 8TX**

⚲ NN 096 084

⌂ Church of Scotland

🌐 www.inveraraychurch.org.uk

Centrepiece of the planned town, this classical church was designed by Robert Mylne in 1792 to house two congregations, English and Gaelic, each with its own entrance under its own portico. The tower with spire rises from the solid wall which separated the two identical halves. Gaelic portion converted to church hall, 1957. Chamber organ by David Hamilton of Edinburgh, 1840s. Furnishings, including the screen and pulpit, were installed in 1898.

- Sunday: 11.15am
- Open July and August (ask at church hall) (01499 302153)

26 ALL SAINTS' CHURCH AND BELL-TOWER, INVERARAY

**The Avenue
Inveraray
PA32 8YX**

⚲ NN 095 085

⌂ Scottish Episcopal, Roman Catholic

🌐 www.argyllandtheisles.org.uk/ inveraray.html

Linked with Christ Church, Lochgilphead (41), St Columba's, Poltalloch (47)

Gothic-style church built 1885 in local red granite, designed by Wardrop and Anderson of Edinburgh. Many of the interior furnishings given by Niall Diarmid, 10th Duke of Argyll. Bell-tower, in Gothic Revival by Hoare & Wheeler, built 1923–31 as a memorial to Campbell dead of First World War and previous wars. Peal of ten bells by John Taylor of Loughborough, 1926. Exhibition in entrance to ringing chamber.

- Scottish Episcopal: 2nd Sunday of the month, 3.00pm; Roman Catholic: 12.30pm every Sunday
- Open daily, early April to end September (01546 602315)

 (church) (bell-tower)

27 KILBERRY PARISH CHURCH

Kilberry
PA29 6YB

⚔ NR 741 620

🏠 Church of Scotland

Linked with Tarbert (50)

19km (12 miles) from Tarbert on B8024

The church was built in 1821. Plain oblong building, galleries on three sides. Later alterations provided an internal stair and removed the original external access.

- Sunday: fortnightly, summer 10.00am, winter 2.00pm
- Open daily (01880 820310)

28 KILCALMONELL PARISH CHURCH

Clachan Church

Clachan
Tarbert
PA29 6XL

⚔ NR 763 561

🏠 Church of Scotland

Linked with Killean & Kilchenzie (31)

Just off A83

Clachan was the ancient seat of the Church in North Kintyre. The present traditional harled oblong kirk of around 1760 replaced an earlier church on the site. The church was enlarged in 1828, remodelled in 1878 and the interior refurnished in 1900. The porch was added in 1952. The graveyard contains early Christian, medieval and post-Reformation stones. War Memorial gateway, 1921, by Ebenezer James MacRae.

- Sunday: 10.00am
- Open daily (01583 421249)

29 KILCHRENAN PARISH CHURCH

**Kilchrenan
PA35 1HD**

NN 037 229

Church of Scotland

Linked with Dalavich (15), Muckairn (44)

B845, by Loch Awe

Built in 1770 on the site of an earlier church dating back to the 12th century. Some stones from that church have been incorporated into the present building. Interior remodelled 1904 when the original east–west orientation was re-established. There are interesting tombstones in the graveyard, including that of Cailean Mor (Sir Colin Campbell) in 1294.

- Sunday: 10.00am on 1st, 3rd and 5th Sunday of the month
- Open daily (01866 822677)

B

30 KILFINAN PARISH CHURCH

West Cowal Parish

**Kilfinan
Tighnabruaich
PA21 2EP**

NR 934 789

Church of Scotland

www.drumcot.org

Linked with Colintraive (10), Kilmodan (34)

6.5km (4 miles) south of Otter Ferry on B8000

White-harled T-plan church with foundations from 1235. The church was rebuilt in 1759, incorporating the Lamont Vault of 1633. Renovated by John Honeyman in 1882, giving the church interior and layout we see today. Stones and monuments of interest. An extensive restoration of the building was completed in 2004. The church has important links with the Clan Lamont and the Clan McEwen.

- Sunday: 12.15pm
- Open daily (01700 821207)

B   (guided tours by arrangement)

31 KILLEAN & KILCHENZIE PARISH CHURCH

Cleit Church

**A' Chleit
Muasdale
by Tarbert
PA29 6XD**

Ⓐ NR 681 418

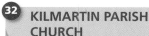 Church of Scotland

Linked with Kilcalmonell (28)

A83, 1.6km (1 mile) north of Muasdale, Kintyre

The church, probably built 1787–91 by Thomas Cairns, is set on a promontory. The exterior is white-harled with round-arched windows. Belfry added 1879 by Robert Weir. The pulpit, in the long west wall, is a First World War memorial with Celtic-style carving, and faces a large laird's loft which has its own separate entrance. Beside the pulpit is a marble monument of 1818 to Col. Norman Macalister, who donated to the poor of the parish. The north gallery was converted into meeting rooms and storage in the early 1970s.

- Sunday: 11.30am
- Open daily (01583 421249)

32 KILMARTIN PARISH CHURCH

**Kilmartin
PA31 8RQ**

Ⓐ NR 835 989

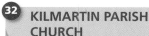 Church of Scotland

🌐 http://argyllcommunities.org/
glassarykilmartinford/services/

A816, 13km (8 miles) north of Lochgilphead

On the site of earlier churches, the present building opened in 1835. The architect was James Gordon Davis. Three interesting memorial panels from the 18th and 19th centuries to members of the family of Campbell of Duntroon. The church has two outstanding early Christian crosses. The kirkyard contains the mausoleum of Bishop Neil Campbell and medieval tomb-slabs. Extensive views over Bronze Age burial cairns.

- Sunday: 10.00am every 3rd Sunday in even-numbered years, 11.30am every 3rd Sunday in odd-numbered years
- Open daily, 9.30am–4.00pm (01546 810286)

33 KILMELFORD PARISH CHURCH

**Kilmelford
PA34 4XA**

⚐ NM 849 130

⛪ Church of Scotland

Linked with Craignish (12), Kilninver (37), Kilchattan, Luing (65), Kilbrandon, Seil (67)

At junction of A816 and road to Loch Avich

Small, attractive building of 1785, reroofed 1890. Oblong plan with gable front with 'birdcage' belfry and 8-spoked wheel window over pointed arch entrance. Plain, tall interior with open timber roof. Balcony with spiral stair with barley-sugar balusters. Pulpit box. Major repairs, 2008–10.

- Sunday: fortnightly 12.00 noon, alternating with Kilninver
- Open daily, enter through vestry (01852 200565)

34 KILMODAN CHURCH

West Cowal Parish

**Glendaruel
PA22 3AA**

⚐ NR 995 842

⛪ Church of Scotland

Linked with Colintraive (10), Kilfinan (30)

Clachan of Glendaruel, A886

A Georgian T-plan church of 1783 on the site of an earlier church of 1610. Completely restored in 1983. Segmental-arched windows; lofts in the three arms. Handsome and elegant interior with two long narrow communion tables. Memorial to Rev. John Maclaurin and his two famous sons (Colin was author of Maclaurin's mathematical theorem).

- Sunday: 10.00am or 11.30am, alternating monthly with Colintraive
- Open daily (01369 820232)

35 KILMORICH PARISH CHURCH

Cairndow
PA26 8BA

⚐ NN 181 107

⛪ Church of Scotland

Head of Loch Fyne

Pyramidal-roofed octagon with square tower with traceried parapet and corner finials, commissioned by Sir Andrew Campbell and built by Andrew McKindley in 1816. The rubble masonry is white-harled with ashlar sandstone eaves and door and window surrounds. The octagonal shape is reflected in the interior.

- Sunday: 12.15pm
- Open daily (01301 703059)

36 KILMUN PARISH CHURCH

St Munn's

Kilmun
PA23 8TE

⚐ NS 166 821

⛪ Church of Scotland

🌐 www.cowalshorechurches.org.uk

Linked with Ardentinny (4), Strone (49)

A880, on Holy Loch

On the site of a Celtic monastery, overlooking Holy Loch. Tower of 15th-century collegiate church. Present building dates from 1841, by Thomas Burns with interior remodelled by Peter Macgregor Chalmers in 1899. Important stained glass by Stephen Adam and Alfred Webster. Water-powered organ by Norman & Beard, 1909. Ancient graveyard with fine 18th-century carved stones. Mausoleum of Dukes of Argyll, Douglas vault. Grave of Elizabeth Blackwell, first lady doctor.

- Sunday: 12.00 noon
- Open May to end September, Tuesday to Thursday 1.30–4.30pm (last tour 4.00pm); or by arrangement (01369 840313)

ARGYLL & BUTE

37 KILNINVER PARISH CHURCH

**Kilninver
PA34 4UT**

⚔ NM 825 217

⛪ Church of Scotland

Linked with Craignish (12), Kilmelford (33), Kilchattan, Luing (65), Kilbrandon, Seil (67)

At junction of A816 and B844 to Seil

Christian worship was recorded at Kilninver in the 1200s. The present simple country church of 1793 is by John Clark, mason, of Oban – oblong in plan with 'birdcage' belfry. Radically reconstructed in 1892 when the porch and vestry were added and the windows altered. Panelled rear gallery and pitch-pine pulpit box. Major repairs, 2005–8.

- Sunday: fortnightly 12.00 noon, alternating with Kilmelford
- Open by arrangement (01852 200565)

38 ST CONAN'S KIRK, LOCHAWE

**Lochawe
PA33 1AH**

⚔ NN 116 268

⛪ Ecumenical

🌐 www.loch-awe.com/local_groups/stconanskirk.htm

North end of Loch Awe, on A85

A labour of love by Walter Campbell of Innis Chonain. The nave and choir were built 1881–6, and the church was extended and embellished 1907–30. An astonishing building, rich in detail, mostly in Romanesque style, although Walter Campbell 'did not allow himself to be trammelled by orthodoxy'. Overlooking Loch Awe in a place of great natural beauty.

- Church of Scotland: 9.00am on 1st Sunday of the month
- Open daily (01838 200298)

39 LOCHFYNESIDE PARISH CHURCH

Minard
PA32 8YB

⚓ NR 978 962

⛪ Church of Scotland

Linked with Cumlodden (14), Lochgair (40)

On A83, 8km (5 miles) south-west of Furnace

Good example of a corrugated-iron church by Speirs & Co. of Glasgow, 'Designers and Erectors of Iron and Wood Buildings', 1910. Stained-glass window by Sax Shaw, 1984. Pulpit of ancient ash from Crarae estate, designed by Ilay M. Campbell.

- Sunday: 12.00 noon, except 4th Sunday of the month
- Open by arrangement (01499 500288)

Gaelic

40 LOCHGAIR PARISH CHURCH

Lochgair
PA31 8SB

⚓ NR 922 905

⛪ Church of Scotland

Linked with Cumlodden (14), Lochfyneside (39)

On A83 between Furnace and Lochgilphead

Originally a mission church of Glassary parish. Built 1867 to a simple oblong design with pointed windows and whitewashed walls. Half-octagon box pulpit centred between blind lancets.

- Sunday: 3.00pm on 1st, 2nd and 3rd Sunday of the month; Gaelic Service 3.00pm on 2nd Sunday of the month
- Open daily (01499 500288)

Gaelic

41 CHRIST CHURCH, LOCHGILPHEAD

**Bishopton Road
Lochgilphead
PA31 8PY**

A NR 860 884

Scottish Episcopal

⊕ www.argyllandtheisles.org.uk/
lochgilphead.html

Linked with All Saints', Inveraray (26), St Columba's, Poltalloch (47)

On the Oban road out of Lochgilphead

An Episcopalian congregation was first gathered for worship at Lochgilphead in 1842. The church and adjoining rectory were designed by John Henderson in 1850–1. Nave-and-chancel church with an arch-braced nave roof. Organ chamber built 1887–8 to house the organ by William Hill & Son, 1876.

- Sunday: 9.00am (except 1st Sunday of the month) and 11.00am
- Open daily (01546 602315)

42 LOCHGOILHEAD & KILMORICH PARISH CHURCH

**Lochgoilhead
PA24 8AA**

A NN 198 015

Church of Scotland

On B839

Dedicated to the Three Holy Brethren, the church is first mentioned in papal letters of 1379. It was rebuilt as a T-plan kirk in the 18th century, incorporating the medieval walls and the 16th-century Ardkinglas monument. The interior was refurbished by Ian G. Lindsay in 1957, retaining the historical layout and incorporating an 18th-century pulpit. Many features of interest.

- Sunday: 10.30am
- Open daily (01301 703059)

43 LUSS PARISH CHURCH

St Mackessog's

**Luss
G83 8NZ**

🅰 NS 361 929

⛪ Church of Scotland

🌐 www.lussonline.net

On the banks of Loch Lomond, off A82

This picturesque church of 1875, the third built on this site on the banks of Loch Lomond, with its beautiful stained-glass windows and uniquely timbered roof, featured frequently in TV's *Take the High Road*. Cruciform church in Decorated Gothic style with a belfry at the crossing. The graveyard has 15 listed ancient monuments.

- Sunday: 11.45am
- Open daily 10.00am to dusk (01436 860240)

44 MUCKAIRN PARISH CHURCH

Taynuilt
PA35 1JN

🅰 NN 005 310

⛪ Church of Scotland

Linked with Dalavich (15), Kilchrenan (29)

On A85

Built in 1829, the church stands adjacent to the ruins (1228) of Killespickerill, once the seat of the Bishop of Argyll. Typical rural kirk of the reformed tradition: rectangular with large round-headed windows and a bellcote. Two stones of antiquity are built into the walls of the present church. Tombstones from the 14th century can be seen in the graveyard.

- Sunday: 11.30am
- Open daylight hours (01866 822677)

45 CATHEDRAL CHURCH OF ST JOHN THE DIVINE, OBAN

**George Street
Oban
PA34 5NY**

A NM 859 304

Scottish Episcopal

⊕ www.argyllandtheisles.org.uk/
oban.html

Linked with St James's,
Ardbrecknish (3)

The cathedral is a small part of the
projected building, consisting of
chancel, crossing, nave of one bay
and one transept by James Chalmers,
1908, attached at right angles to the
existing church by Charles Wilson
and David Thomson, giving an
extraordinary building internally.
Tall reredos on a Scottish theme
with painting of the Ascension set
in the West Highlands, by Norman
Macdougall. Vast hovering bronze
eagle. Choir stalls in form of Celtic
graveyard. Much Iona marble and
terrazzo.

- Sunday: 8.00am, 10.15am;
  Wednesday: 11.00am
- Open daily (01631 562323)

46 ST COLUMBA'S CATHEDRAL, OBAN

**Corran Esplanade
Oban
PA34 5AB**

A NM 855 307

Roman Catholic

Built between 1932 and 1958, St
Columba's Cathedral is the principal
church of the Roman Catholic Diocese
of Argyll and the Isles. Designed by
Giles Gilbert Scott in the neo-Gothic
style, of highly distinctive, lofty, pink
granite. The tower soars above the
Esplanade. High timber reredos with
intricate Gothic fretwork, designed by
Scott and carved by Donald Gilbert.

- Saturday: 7.00pm; Sunday: 10.30am
- Open daily (01631 562123)

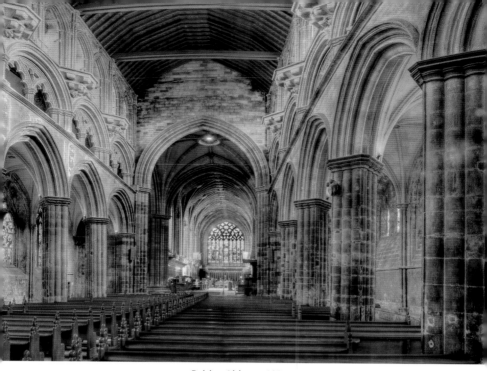

Paisley Abbey   102

Trinity Parish Church, Bute   51

St John's Church, Dunoon   19

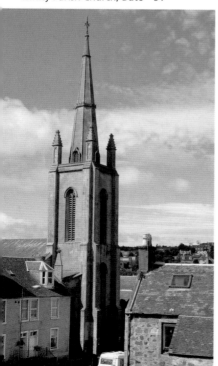

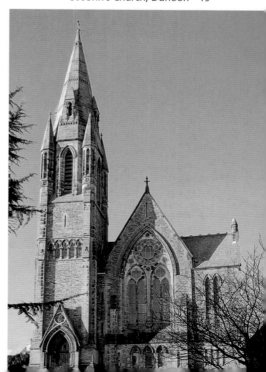

St Bartholomew's, Gourock   71

St Patrick's, Greenock   76

Johnstone High Parish Church   98

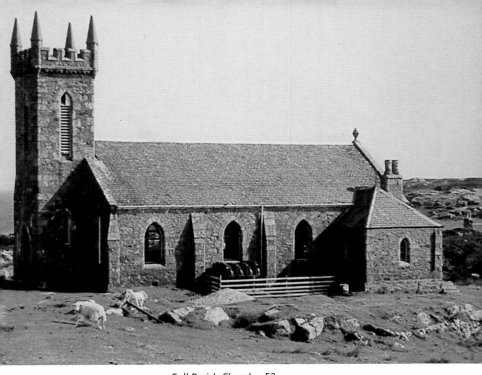

Coll Parish Church   53

Kilchrenan Parish Church   29

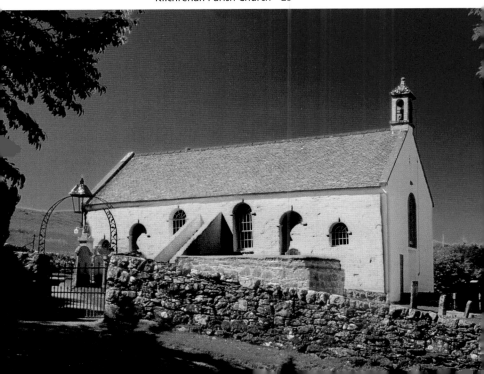

The United Church of Bute   52

Kilmorich Parish Church   35

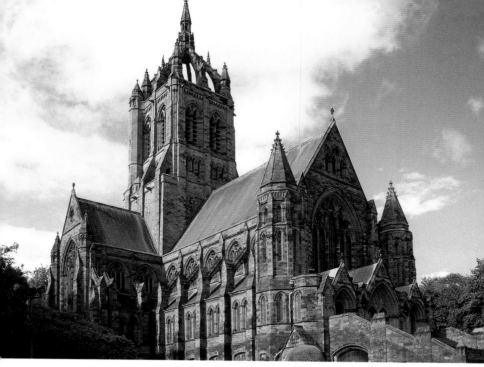

Thomas Coats Memorial Baptist Church, Paisley 106

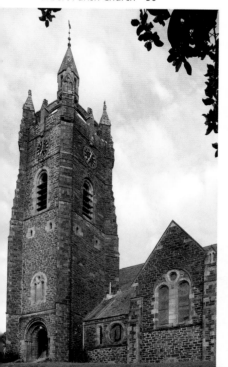

Greenock West United Reformed Church   85

St Columba's Cathedral, Oban   46

Paisley Abbey   102

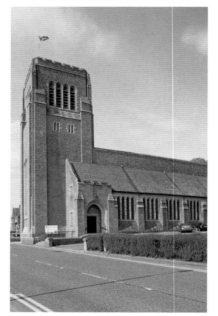

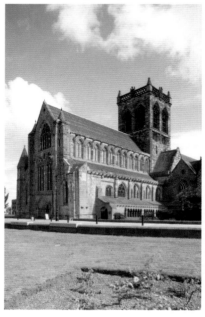

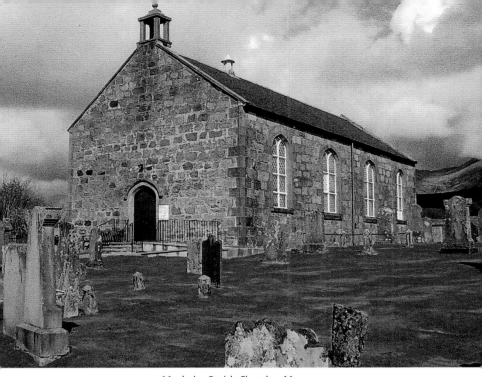

Muckairn Parish Church   44

St James's Church, Paisley   105

St John's, Gourock   72

St Francis's, Port Glasgow   92

47 ST COLUMBA'S, POLTALLOCH

**Poltalloch Estate
Kilmartin
PA31 8QF**

🅰 NR 816 965

⛪ Scottish Episcopal

🌐 www.scotland.anglican.org/
kilmartin.htm

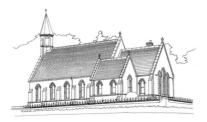

Linked with All Saints', Inveraray
(26), Christ Church, Lochgilphead
(41)

3km (2 miles) south-west of Kilmartin

In the gentle parkland of ruined
Poltalloch House (William Burn,
1849), St Columba's was conceived as
a private chapel but built as a church
with congregation and incumbent.
Built 1852 to a design by William
Cundy of London in Early English
style with leafy carvings and pointed
arches. Complete set of stained glass
by William Wailes. Organ by Gray
& Davison, 1855. Two Whitechapel
Foundry bells. Three misericord seats.

- Sunday: 9.00am on 1st Sunday
  of the month, 3.30pm on 3rd
  Sunday
- Open daily (01546 602519)

 B

48 ST MODAN'S PARISH CHURCH, ROSNEATH

**Rosneath Road
Rosneath
G84 0RQ**

🅰 NS 255 832

⛪ Church of Scotland

Linked with Craigrownie (13)

On B833

There has been a church at Rosneath
since the time of St Modan c. AD
600–50. The present building, 1853, is
by architect David Cousin. The bell
by Jan Burgerhuis, 1610, on display
in the present building, was rung as
a summons to arms during the 1715
Jacobite Rebellion. Organ by Hill, 1875.
Reredos of the Ten Commandments
by W. A. Muirhead and the Last
Supper by Meredith Williams, carved
by Thomas Wood. Mural of St Modan
by Mary Ainsworth, 1995. Stained
glass by Clayton & Bell, Douglas
Strachan, Stephen Adam & Co.,
Gordon Webster, Crear McCartney.

- Sunday: 10.00am in odd-numbered
  years, 11.30am in even-numbered
  years
- Open by arrangement (01436 831763)

   (by arrangement)

49 STRONE CHURCH

St Columba's

**Shore Road
Strone
PA23 8TB**

⚐ NS 193 806

⛪ Church of Scotland

🌐 www.cowalshorechurches.org.uk

Linked with Ardentinny (4), Kilmun (36)

A880, on Holy Loch

The square, battlemented tower and spire survive of the original 1858 church and are used as a navigation aid for shipping. The rest of the building 1907–8 by Peter Macgregor Chalmers, using material from the old church. Stained glass by Stephen Adam and Gordon Webster.

- Sunday: 10.30am
- Open daily (01369 840313)

50 TARBERT PARISH CHURCH

**Campbeltown Road
Tarbert
PA29 6TU**

⚐ NR 863 686

⛪ Church of Scotland

Linked with Kilberry (27)

Built in 1886 on the site of an earlier mission church dating from 1775 and granted quoad sacra status in 1864. Architects J. McKissack and W. G. Rowan of Glasgow. The building features an imposing square tower rising over 30 metres (100ft), surmounted by a crown and lantern. Stained-glass windows and unusual roof decoration.

- Sunday: 11.30am
- Open April to September, 10.00am–5.30pm (01880 820310)

51 TRINITY PARISH CHURCH, BUTE

**Castle Street
Rothesay
Isle of Bute
PA20 9HA**

NS 089 645

Church of Scotland

www.isle-of-bute.com/trinity/

Opened as the Free Church in 1845. Designed by Archibald Simpson in severe Gothic with a square tower surmounted with a slender spire. The interior, in contrast, is softened by the warmth of the hammer-beam roof and colourful stained-glass windows by Oscar Paterson and Gordon Webster.

- Sunday: 11.00am; 6.30pm on 1st Sunday of the month
- Open by arrangement (01700 503010)

52 THE UNITED CHURCH OF BUTE

formerly Rothesay High Kirk

**High Street
Rothesay
Isle of Bute
PA20 9HA**

NS 086 637

Church of Scotland

www.unitedchurchofbute.org.uk

Designed by Adam Russell and built in 1796, this is the third church on this site. Remodelled by John Russell Thomson in 1905–6 with U-plan gallery. Eight stained-glass windows by Stephen Adam and D. Hamilton. A new church centre (adjoining the existing church building) has recently been constructed.

- Sunday: 11.00am
- Open by arrangement (07732 548566)

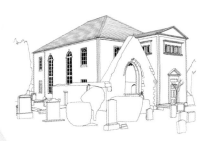

53 COLL PARISH CHURCH

**Arinagour
Isle of Coll
PA72 6SY**

⚔ NM 224 574

⛪ Church of Scotland

🌐 www.connelchurch.co.uk/

Linked with Connel (11), Dunbeg (16)

Footpath beside Coll Hotel

Prominently sited on a hill at the head of Loch Eatharna overlooking the village of Arinagour. A rectangular Gothic-style church with buttresses and a square bell-tower, designed by Robert Robertson and built in 1907. The Arts & Crafts-style well-crafted herring-bone patterned timber roof is a high-quality and rare design. Clear glass windows give spectacular sea views.

- Sunday: 11.30am, Easter to September; monthly in winter
- Open daily (01879 230366)

54 COLONSAY & ORONSAY PARISH CHURCH

**Scalasaig
Isle of Colonsay
PA61 7YW**

⚔ NR 390 941

⛪ Church of Scotland

By Scalasaig ferry terminal

Built in 1802 to the design of architect Michael Carmichael. The kirk originally had galleries at both ends, accessed by extranal staircases. Features include a 'birdcage' belfry and round-headed windows. Well-lit interior graced by an attractive combed wooden ceiling. One incumbent (1917–25) was Kenneth MacLeod, who wrote the song 'The Road to the Isles'.

- Sunday: 11.30am, alternating weekly with Baptist Church, Kilchattan
- Open daily (01951 200320)

55 GIGHA & CARA PARISH CHURCH

**Ardminish
Isle of Gigha
PA41 7AA**

⚔ NR 648 489

⛪ Church of Scotland

Built 1923. Designed by architect-minister Donald MacFarlane in a Romanesque Revival style with round-headed windows. Windows by William Wilson and Gordon Webster. First minister was Dr Kenneth MacLeod, who wrote 'The Road to the Isles'. Stone baptismal font from Kilchattan Church.

- Sunday: 11.00am
- Open daily

56 IONA ABBEY

**Isle of Iona
PA76 6SQ**

⚔ NM 287 245

⛪ Ecumenical

🌐 www.historic-scotland.gov.uk

On the original site of St Columba's monastery, c. AD 563. St Columba's Shrine dates from the 9th century, and most of the present buildings from c. 1200. The restoration of the Abbey Church was completed in 1910. The Iona Community now occupies the monastic buildings. Imposing standing crosses and one of the largest collections of early Christian carved stones in Europe.

- March to November: Sunday 10.30am and 9.00pm, Monday to Saturday 2.00pm and 9.00pm; December to February: Monday to Saturday 9.00pm
- Open 9.30am–5.00pm, 1 April to 30 September; 9.30am–4.00pm 1 October to 31 March (01681 700512)

ARGYLL & BUTE

57 IONA PARISH CHURCH

Isle of Iona
PA76 6SJ

NM 285 243

Church of Scotland

www.argyllandtheisles.org.uk/iona.html

A Thomas Telford church of 1828. Pews, pulpit and communion table realigned in 1939. Former manse of same date now a heritage centre with picnic area adjacent.

- Sunday: 12.00 noon
- Open daily

58 KILMENY PARISH CHURCH, ISLAY

Ballygrant
Isle of Islay
PA45 7QW

NR 353 636

Church of Scotland

www.islay-north-churches.org

Remodelled in 1828 to plans by Thomas Telford, and standing about 400 metres north-east of its medieval predecessor. The interior has recently been upgraded with comfortable seating both on pews and on padded chairs.

- Sunday: 10.00am
- Open July to August, Thursday 2.00–4.00pm (01496 810236)

 (Thursdays in July and August)

Gaelic

59 KILARROW PARISH CHURCH, BOWMORE, ISLAY

The Round Church

**Main Street
Bowmore
Isle of Islay
PA43 7JD**

NR 312 596

Church of Scotland

www.theroundchurch.org.uk

Linked with St John's, Port Ellen (61)

This 18th-century church, known as 'the Round Church', was built by Daniel Campbell of Shawfield and Islay in 1767. The two-storey circular body of the church has a main central pillar of wood 19 inches in diameter, harled and plastered. The gallery was added in 1830. Extensive recent renovations.

- Sunday: 10.00am
- Open daily 9.00am–6.00pm (01496 810271)

 (Tuesday and Thursday in summer)

60 ST KIARAN'S, PORT CHARLOTTE, ISLAY

**Port Charlotte
Isle of Islay
PA48 7UD**

NR 257 594

Church of Scotland

www.islay-north-churches.org

Linked with Portnahaven (62)

On A847

Designed by Peter Macgregor Chalmers and constructed 1897 in Romanesque style in rubble stone dressed with red sandstone. Conical roofed apse. Centenary tapestry on display.

- Sunday: 11.30am
- Open daily (01496 850241)

Gaelic

61 **ST JOHN'S CHURCH, PORT ELLEN, ISLAY**

Kildalton & Oa Parish Church

**Port Ellen
Isle of Islay
PA42 7DH**

NR 367 451

Church of Scotland

Linked with Kilarrow, Bowmore (59)

Situated in a prominent position facing Loch Leodamais in the planned village of Port Ellen. Small, single-storey rectangular plan, Arts & Crafts church by Sydney Mitchell, 1898. Broached spire. Carved oak font, lectern and communion table with Gothic panels. Lancet windows with foliated tracery. Stained glass of Christ the Good Shepherd and fishing and harvest scenes.

- Sunday: 11.30am and 7.00pm
- Open daily (01496 302440)

62 **PORTNAHAVEN PARISH CHURCH, ISLAY**

**Portnahaven
Isle of Islay
PA47 7SW**

NR 168 523

Church of Scotland

www.islay-north-churches.org

Linked with St Kiaran's, Port Charlotte (60)

A Telford Parliamentary kirk built in 1828 by William Thompson. T-plan with north, east and west galleries. The symmetrical south front has two tall four-centred arched windows and two doorways. Legend has it that one door is used by Portnahaven residents exclusively, the other door by residents of nearby Port Wemyss.

- Sunday: 10.00am
- Open daily (01496 860214)

Gaelic

ARGYLL & BUTE

63 JURA PARISH CHURCH

Craighouse
Isle of Jura
PA60 7YA

NR 527 677

Church of Scotland

The harled church was built in 1776. Pennant in his *Voyage to the Hebrides* (1776) says 'land in Jura, at a little village, and see to the right on the shore the church, and the minister's manse'. Alterations 1842 and 1922. Superb photographic exhibition of 'Old Jura' in an upper gallery reached by an external stair behind the church.

- Sunday: 11.30am
- Open daily (01496 820351)

64 THE CATHEDRAL CHURCH OF SAINT MOLUAG, LISMORE

Lismore Parish Church

Clachan
Isle of Lismore
PA34 5UL

NM 861 435

Church of Scotland

3km (2 miles) north of pier

The Cathedral Church of Saint Moluag was built in the 14th century and attributed locally, by tradition, to 'the Roman' or 'an Ròmhanach'. Medieval carved slab-stones, said to be of the 'Loch Awe' school, and recumbent carved stone within the building. Traditional baptismal font carved in a natural rock surface in the graveyard. Piscina and triple sedilia are a lovely feature, the floor now 0.6 metres higher than in medieval times.

- Sunday: 12.30pm
- Open daily (01631 760257)

   (by arrangement)

65 KILCHATTAN CHURCH, LUING

**Toberonochy
Isle of Luing
PA34 4TY**

NM 743 104

Church of Scotland

Linked with Craignish (12), Kilmelford (33), Kilninver (37), Kilbrandon, Seil (67)

Just beyond the school on the road to Toberonochy

Simple white-painted rectangular church built in 1936. The church houses a beautifully carved, floor-standing wooden lectern and two wooden offering plates donated by Latvian ship-owners to mark the rescue efforts of the islanders when one of their ships foundered in a storm on the island of Belnahua in 1938.

• Sunday: 11.30am
• Open daily (01852 314230)

66 KILMORE CHURCH, MULL

**Dervaig
Isle of Mull
PA75 6QW**

NM 432 517

Church of Scotland

Opened in June 1905 on the site of an earlier church, architect Peter Macgregor Chalmers. Simple exterior with 'pencil' tower. The interior is in the Arts & Crafts style and features a painted apse and characteristically plain but beautiful pulpit and communion table. Significant stained glass by Stephen Adam.

• Sunday: 2.00pm
• Open daily (01688 400310)

67 KILBRANDON CHURCH, SEIL

Balvicar
Isle of Seil
PA34 4RJ

NM 758 155

Church of Scotland

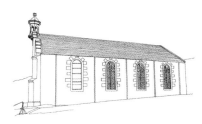

Linked with Craignish (12), Kilmelford (33), Kilninver (37), Kilchattan, Luing (65)

On B8003, 1.6km (1 mile) south of the Balvicar turn-off

Simple hall-church built in 1866 by Alexander McIntyre. The kirk contains a beautiful set of five stained-glass windows, the work of Douglas Strachan. The windows were commissioned by Miss Mackinnon of Ardmaddy Castle in 1937 in memory of her friend the Marchioness of Breadalbane.

- Sunday: 10.00am, except last Sunday of the month 11.00am
- Open daily (01852 314230)

68 HEYLIPOL CHURCH, TIREE

Barrapol
Isle of Tiree
PA77 6XJ

NL 964 432

Church of Scotland

Linked with Kirkapol (69)

B8065

The distinctiveness of Heylipol church or Eaglais na Mointeach, 'the church of the moss', is enhanced by its location at a crossroads in a stretch of open country. Built 1902 by architect William MacKenzie of Oban, in cruciform Gothic with a bell-tower over the porch.

- Sunday: 11.30am and 6.00pm, alternating with Kirkapol Church
- Open daily (01879 220377)

Gaelic

69 KIRKAPOL CHURCH, TIREE

**Kirkapol
Gott Bay
Isle of Tiree
PA77 6TN**

⚲ NM 041 468

🏛 Church of Scotland

Linked with Heylipol (68)

B8068

The current church of Kirkapol (Norse for 'church town') is a continuing witness to the Christian faith that stretches back to Columban times. Built in 1842 by architect-contractor Peter MacNab as a simple square box. Galleries on three sides focus on a central pulpit at the centre of the north wall. Some of the granite came from the same quarry as that for the Skerryvore lighthouse.

- Sunday: 11.30am and 6.00pm, alternating with Heylipol Church
- Open daily (01879 220377)

Gaelic

70 ST NINIAN'S, GOUROCK

**18 Royal Street
Gourock
PA19 1PN**

⚲ NS 242 777

🏛 Roman Catholic

Chapel-school of 1878, extended in 1982 for the visit to Scotland of Pope John Paul II – the altar contains marble from the papal altar at Bellahouston. Mosaics by Frank Tritschler, stained glass by Dom Ninian Sloan of Pluscarden Abbey, and a chasuble fashioned from an original Paisley shawl by Debbie Gonet. Small museum.

- Saturday: 5.30pm; Sunday: 9.30am and 11.30am; weekdays: 10.00am
- Open daily 9.00am–6.00pm (01475 632078)

71 ST BARTHOLOMEW'S, GOUROCK

**Barrhill Road
Gourock
PA19 1JX**

NS 239 777

Scottish Episcopal

Linked with St John's, Greenock (78)

This beautiful little church sits on a cliff overlooking the River Clyde. Designed by J. C. Sharp of Gourock, 1857. Chancel extension enhanced by a beautiful window depicting the Ascension by George Walton. Mural of the Nativity on the west wall. Plaque of Dutch tiles in remembrance of the hospitality given to Dutch soldiers, sailors and airmen during the Second World War.

- Sunday and Wednesday: 10.30am
- Open by arrangement (01475 732441)

72 ST JOHN'S, GOUROCK

**Bath Street
Gourock
PA19 1LA**

NS 241 778

Church of Scotland

www.stjohnschurchgourock.co.uk

Gothic-style church built 1857 (J. J. and W. H. Hay), and tower with open-work crown added 1878 (Bruce & Sturrock). The sanctuary underwent major renovations in 1998, when wooden flooring was laid and the pews were replaced by chairs to give greater flexibility. Makin organ. Lively and quiet worship when we can come together to praise and glorify God. The church is used daily by many organisations.

- Sunday: 11.00am
- Open by arrangement (01475 630879)

73 OLD GOUROCK AND ASHTON PARISH CHURCH

**41 Royal Street
Gourock
PA19 1PW**

⚔ NS 243 775

🏛 Church of Scotland

🌐 www.ogachurch.org.uk

Congregation is the 1989 union of Old Gourock Parish and Ashton Parish Church in the building of the former, opened 1832 and enlarged 1872 and 1900. Dominant square crenallated tower on entrance façade. Pulpit and choir stall with panels by C. R. Mackintosh, 1900. Twelve stained-glass windows, four by Gordon Webster. Sculpture by George Wyllie. Allen computer organ, 1991.

- Sunday: 9.30am and 11.00am; 10.00am only July and first two Sundays in August
- Open by arrangement (01475 659276)

74 OLD WEST KIRK, GREENOCK

**Esplanade
Greenock
PA16 8AN**

⚔ NS 273 772

🏛 Church of Scotland

🌐 www.owkgreenock.info/

Cruciform church first built 1591 at Westburn, but rebuilt here 1926–8 with a new tower designed by James Miller. Also brought from the old site are the surrounding headstones and grave-slabs, some bearing trade emblems or coats of arms. Inside the church are galleries originally intended to be occupied by the laird, the sailors and the farmers of the parish. Stained glass by Morris, Marshall & Faulkner and Daniel Cottier. Behind the octagonal pulpit is a mural panel by local artist Ian Philips, 1991.

- Sunday: 11.00am
- Open Wednesday, mid-May to mid-September, 10.30am–12.00 noon (01475 729800)

75 ARDGOWAN PARISH CHURCH, GREENOCK

Trinity Church, St Andrew's Church

31 Union Street Greenock PA16 8DD

 NS 271 768

 Church of Scotland

Between Robertson Street and Campbell Street

Built as Trinity United Presbyterian Church, 1871, and designed by John Starforth in Gothic style with a square tower. Became St Andrews in 1967 when united with St Andrews, and Ardgowan in 1992 when united with Union Church. Galleried interior refurbished in 2002 after the ceiling collapsed.

- Sunday: 11.00am
- Open by arrangement (01475 722694)

76 ST PATRICK'S, GREENOCK

5 Orangefield Place Greenock PA15 1YX

 NS 271 761

 Roman Catholic

 www.stpatricksgreenock.org.uk

Striking example of the work of G. Antonio Coia, 1935. The soaring gable characterises a church of great strength. A framework of steel is encased in reinforced concrete and enveloped in red Lancashire brick with a backing of Scots clay cement bricks. Exquisite stone sculpture by Archibald Dawson, including bas-relief of St Patrick blessing a child, rising from between the two doors.

- Saturday: 7.00pm; Sunday: 8.00am, 10.00am, 11.30am and 7.00pm
- Open daily 8.00am–7.30pm (01475 720223)

77 FINNART ST PAUL'S, GREENOCK

**Newark Street
Greenock
PA16 7UR**

⛰ NS 265 774

⛪ Church of Scotland

🌐 www.finnart-stpauls-church.org

Finely detailed late Gothic church designed by Sir Robert Rowand Anderson and opened for public worship in 1893. Nave-and-chancel church in red sandstone with a lofty interior lit by clerestory windows. Stained glass by Burne-Jones, Douglas Strachan and William Wilson. 3-manual and pedal pipe organ by 'Father' Willis, 1894.

- Sunday: 11.00am
- Open by arrangement (01475 639602)

    (by arrangement)
 (by arrangement)

78 ST JOHN THE EVANGELIST, GREENOCK

**Union Street
Greenock
PA16 8JJ**

⛰ NS 274 766

⛪ Scottish Episcopal

🌐 http://stjohnsgreenock.co.uk/

Linked with St Bartholomew's, Gourock (71)

Opposite Watt Library

The present building was consecrated in 1878, designed by Paley and Austin of Lancaster – their only Scottish church. The intricately carved rood screen, based on a medieval screen in Gloucestershire and designed by H. O. Tarbolton, was given by the family of Sir John Kerr, one-time Governor of Bengal. The font is a copy of a 15th-century font in Suffolk. Organ by J. & A. Mirrlees of Glasgow.

- Sunday: 8.30am and 11.00am
- Open by arrangement (01475 796331)

79 WESTBURN PARISH CHURCH, GREENOCK

St Luke's

**9 Nelson Street
Greenock
PA15 1TP**

NS 273 763

Church of Scotland

www.greenockwestburn.co.uk

Designed by David Cousin and built in 1840, with the spire added in 1855. The clock was the gift of Miss Frances Ann Wood. The interior was completely gutted by fire in 1912 and replaced by a new chancel, designed by John Keppie, with four stained-glass windows, a new organ and seating for 1,144.

- Sunday: 11.00am
- Open by arrangement (01475 725451)

 (by arrangement)

80 ST MARY'S, GREENOCK

**14 Patrick Street
Greenock
PA16 8NA**

NS 274 768

Roman Catholic

www.stmarysgreenock.org

Designed in Early French Gothic style by George Goldie and opened in 1862. The tower was left incomplete. Major alterations 1914, including a new Lady Chapel. The sanctuary was remodelled in the 1960s and 1970s. Complete renovation in 2003 included new altar, main entrance porch and side door. Stained-glass windows by Wailes of Newcastle and Patrick Feeny.

- Saturday: 6.30pm; Sunday: 10.00am and 12.00 noon; weekdays: 10.00am
- Open daily 9.00am–2.00pm; Sunday 9.00am–4.00pm (01475 721084)

HOLY ROSARY CHAPEL, GREENOCK

**44 Union Street
Greenock
PA16 8DP**

NS 274 765

Roman Catholic

The chapel lies at the heart of each of the Homes of the Little Sisters of the Poor; a place of sanctuary and tranquillity for the sisters, residents and visitors. The residence opened in August 2004, replacing the original residence dating from 1884, offering care for those in need regardless of creed. Stained glass by Susan Bradbury.

- Mass 10.00am daily and 11.00am Sunday
- Open by arrangement (01475 722465)

 GREENOCK METHODIST CHURCH

**Ardgowan Street
Greenock
PA16 8LE**

NS 274 765

Methodist

The roots of this church go back to two visits by John Wesley in 1772 and 1774. The first Wesleyan Methodist Chapel was built in 1814 and replaced by the present building in 1883. Simple church with Gothic details.

- Sunday: 11.00am
- Open Wednesday 10.00am–12.00 noon (01475 722706)

83 GREENOCK EAST UNITED REFORMED CHURCH

**Bawhirley Road
Greenock
PA15 2BH**

NS 292 753

United Reformed Church

Linked with Port Glasgow URC (94)

The current building was designed by Congregational Union architect Fred McDermid and opened in 1968. It is a building of its era with a flat roof. The sanctuary slopes forward in a cinema style.

- Sunday: 9.45am
- Open by arrangement (01475 713974)

84 THE MOUNT KIRK, GREENOCK

**95 Dempster Street
Greenock
PA15 4ED**

NS 270 759

Church of Scotland

www.themountkirk.org.uk

Junction with Murdiston Street

The Mount Kirk is the result of several unions; the present building is the former Mount Pleasant Free Church of 1910. The building is of red sandstone and consists of a large aisleless nave. The interior is fairly plain and functional, relieved by fine wood carving of the pulpit and organ case. Pulpit falls reflect Greenock's industrial past and present.

- Sunday: 11.00am and 7.00pm
- Open by arrangement (01475 722338)

85 GREENOCK WEST UNITED REFORMED CHURCH

**George Square
Greenock
PA15 1QP**

NS 275 765

United Reformed Church

Tudor Gothic church with well-detailed façade, 1839, designed by John Baird I and built at a cost of £3,635. Inside, a vaulted ceiling, fine stained glass and an outstanding pipe organ. The present congregation was formed by the union of George Square and Nelson Street Congregational Churches.

- Sunday: 11.00am
- Open by arrangement (01475 720039)

86 WELLPARK MID KIRK, GREENOCK

The Toon Kirk

**Cathcart Square
Greenock
PA15 1LS**

NS 279 761

Church of Scotland

Known affectionately as 'the Toon Kirk', this is home to a lively congregation which cherishes its building, a handsome classical church with an Ionic portico and steeple modelled on St Martin-in-the-Fields. The interior has galleries on three sides, a pipe organ of 1867 (restored 2008), stained-glass windows, several memorials and marbles and the friendliest welcome.

- Sunday: 11.00am
- Open Thursday and Friday 10.00am–1.00pm; or by arrangement (01475 721741)

87 INVERKIP CHURCH

**Langhouse Road
Inverkip
PA16 0BJ**

NS 210 722
Church of Scotland
www.inverkip.org.uk

North end of Main Street

The church, reputedly designed by Thomas Telford, was erected in 1804–5. The two-storey T-plan building with an open belfry on the front gable is of local dressed sandstone. Inside, there are east and west galleries and a 'laird's loft', all supported on pillars. The pews, refurbished in 1908, are of rare New Zealand kauri pine.

- Sunday: 11.00am, Thursday: 7.00pm
- Open by arrangement (01475 521215)

88 KILMACOLM OLD KIRK

**High Street
Kilmacolm
PA13 4BP**

NS 358 700
Church of Scotland
www.kilmacolmoldkirk.org.uk

A white-painted church with a tower built in 1830 by James Dempster on the site of 13th- and 16th-century churches. The 13th-century chancel is incorporated as the Murray Chapel. South aisle by J. B. Wilson added in 1903. Early 20th-century stained-glass windows by C. E. Moira, Norman Macdougall and Horace Wilkinson. Modern examples by John K. Clark, Lorraine Lamond and Rab MacInnes.

- Sunday: 11.00am
- Open daily 10.00am–4.00pm (01505 872417)

INVERCLYDE

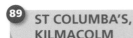

89 ST COLUMBA'S, KILMACOLM

Bridge of Weir Road Kilmacolm PA13 4AS

⋏ NS 358 697

Church of Scotland

Corner of Duchal Road

Built 1901–3 and designed by William Leiper in Decorated Gothic Revival style with a tower with saddle-back roof. Bell by Taylor of Loughborough. Many stained-glass windows, carved stone font, carved oak choir stalls and pulpit and War Memorial panels are all of note. Halls added 1968–9 by Beveridge and Dallachy Architects.

- Sunday: 11.30am (July and August 10.00am) and 6.30pm; Wednesday: 10.30am
- Open by arrangement (0141-887 5821)

90 ST ANDREW'S, PORT GLASGOW

Church Street Port Glasgow PA14 5EH

⋏ NS 320 745

Church of Scotland

A key building in the grid plan of the town. Neo-classical kirk of 1823 with pilastered and pedimented façade topped by a central belfry. Galleried interior, altered 1898 when the chancel was added and the pipe organ installed. Memorial chapel added 1997.

- Sunday: 11.00am
- Open by arrangement (01475 741486)

91 ST MARY THE VIRGIN, PORT GLASGOW

**Bardrainney Avenue
Port Glasgow
PA14 6HB**

A NS 339 733

Scottish Episcopal

Pleasing modern church, 1984, by Frank Burnet, Bell & Partners, incorporating many furnishings and stained-glass windows from the original church of 1857. Stained glass representing characters from the Old Testament, St Mary and Our Lord. The small side chapel, the Epiphany Chapel, has stained glass representing the Three Kings and an icon of the Virgin and Child.

- Sunday: 9.00am and 11.00am; Wednesday: 10.00am; Thursday: 7.00pm
- Open by arrangement (01475 707444)

92 ST FRANCIS'S, PORT GLASGOW

**100 Auchenbothie Road
Port Glasgow
PA14 6JD**

A NS 337 729

Roman Catholic

⊕ www.saintfrancisportglasgow.co.uk

The church opened on 22 December 1974. The sanctuary was refurbished in 1994 with the introduction of the new altar, ambo, tabernacle and font. In 2007, a new Lady Altar was constructed with the original wooden statue as its centrepiece.

- Saturday: 6.00pm; Sunday: 10.30am and 4.30pm
- Open daily 8.30am–4.00pm in winter, 8.30am–8.30pm in summer (01475 700700)

INVERCLYDE

93 ST JOHN THE BAPTIST, PORT GLASGOW

Shore Street
Port Glasgow
PA14 5HD

🄰 NS 319 746

♿ Roman Catholic

🌐 www.stjohnsportglasgow.org.uk

Gothic church built in 1854 with pinnacles rising from the buttressed gable front. Refurbished 2000. Stained glass including 'The Risen Christ' above the main door by Edward Harkness. Fresco of St Thérèse by George Duffy above sacristy door.

- Sunday: 9.30am and 11.00am; Monday, Tuesday, Wednesday and Friday: 9.30am; Thursday: 7:00pm; Saturday: 10.00am and 6.00pm
- Open daily 9.00am–5.00pm (01475 741139)

94 PORT GLASGOW UNITED REFORMED CHURCH

Brown Street
Port Glasgow
PA14 5BP

🄰 NS 319 746

♿ United Reformed Church

Linked with Greenock East URC (83)

The church building, formerly a Temperance Institute, was redesigned by Fred McDermid in 1964 when members moved from the Congregational Union church in Balfour Street. The communion furniture, font and stained-glass window (designed by Charles Hokey) came from the old building (1883).

- Sunday: 11.30am
- Open by arrangement (01475 713974)

95 BISHOPTON PARISH CHURCH

Ferry Road
Bishopton
PA7 5PP

NS 446 720

Church of Scotland

http://bishoptonkirk.org.uk/

On a knoll to the north-east of the village. The Abbey of Paisley founded a church on the site, on the pilgrimage route to Iona, in the 12th century. The current building was constructed in 1812 and is a hall-church with a square tower at the west end.

- Sunday: 11.30am
- Open by arrangement (01505 862583)

96 HOUSTON & KILLELLAN PARISH CHURCH

Kirk Road
Houston
PA6 7HN

NS 411 671

Church of Scotland

www.houstonkirk.org

Between Bridge of Weir and Inchinnan

Designed by David Thomson in 1874, this building is the third on this ancient site. Restored 1938. Early Gothic Revival in style, the church is built in cream sandstone with a square battlemented tower topped with a slated spire. Very good stained glass. Interesting organ.

- Sunday: 11.00am
- Open by arrangement (01505 690690)

RENFREWSHIRE

97 INCHINNAN PARISH CHURCH

St Conval's Kirk

**Old Greenock Road
Inchinnan
Renfrew
PA4 9PH**

⚑ NS 479 689

⛪ Church of Scotland

🌐 www.inchinnanparishchurch.co.uk

Sir Robert Rowand Anderson's church of 1904 was razed to make way for Glasgow Airport, and the present building by Miller and Black, consecrated in 1968, incorporates much of interest and beauty from the earlier church. Foundation by St Conval in AD 597. Celtic and medieval stones.

- Sunday: 10.45am
- Open by arrangement (0141-571 6094)

 (Thursday 11.45am–2.00pm)

98 JOHNSTONE HIGH PARISH CHURCH

**Quarry Street
Johnstone
PA5 8NF**

⚑ NS 426 630

⛪ Church of Scotland

Through shopping arcade from main town square

An octagonal building of grey sandstone built in 1792. The clock-tower with its elegant spire was added in 1823. Stained glass. Historic graveyard.

- Sunday: 11.00am
- Cafe open Thursday and Saturday 10.00am–12.00 noon, all year (01505 342725: Secretary)

   (in halls)

99 KILBARCHAN WEST CHURCH

**Church Street
Kilbarchan
PA10 2JQ**

NS 401 632
Church of Scotland
www.kilbarchanwest.org.uk

Next to NTS Weaver's Cottage

The building that is now the hall was built as the church in 1724 on the site of an earlier church. The present church was completed in 1899–1901, architect W. H. Howie. Some fine stained glass resited from old church and glass from early 20th century. 3-manual organ built 1904 by William Hill & Sons.

- Sunday: 11.00am; Wednesday: 10.30am October to May
- Open by arrangement (01505 342930)

100 KILBARCHAN EAST CHURCH

**Steeple Square
Kilbarchan
PA10 2JD**

NS 404 633
Church of Scotland
www.kilbarchaneastchurch.btik.com

Originally a relief church; foundation stone laid in 1787. Designed by James Brown as a symmetrical two-storey building with a bow front, round-headed windows and piended roof. Interior altered, 1872, by Robert Baldie. Halls added 1931. Two stained-glass windows, one on either side of a large pulpit. Organ by Forster & Andrews.

- Sunday: 11.00am
- Open Tuesday, June to August, 2.00–4.00pm (01505 702670)

101 LINWOOD PARISH CHURCH

**Clippens Road
Linwood
PA3 3PY**

 NS 432 645

Church of Scotland

The first Linwood Parish Church was built in 1860 as a chapel of ease, but it became too small, and the present church was built in 1965. A spacious red-brick building with furniture and communion silver from the earlier church. Contemporary artwork includes a large aluminium cross presented by the former Rootes Vehicle Plant. Fine pipe organ, 1957.

- Sunday: 10.30am
- Open by arrangement (01505 328802)

102 PAISLEY ABBEY

**Abbey Close
Paisley
PA1 1JG**

 NS 486 640

Church of Scotland

www.paisleyabbey.org.uk

Founded in 1163. Early 20th-century restoration of the choir by Peter Macgregor Chalmers and Robert Lorimer. Medieval architecture, 10th-century Barochan Cross and the royal tombs of Marjory Bruce and Robert III. Exceptionally fine woodwork including organ case by Lorimer, stained glass by Burne-Jones and others. Organ by Cavaille-Coll, 1872, rebuilt Walker, 1968.

- Sunday: 11.00am, 12.15pm and 6.30pm
- Open daily, Monday to Saturday 10.00am–3.30pm (0141-889 7654)

103 ST MIRIN'S CATHEDRAL, PAISLEY

Incle Street
Paisley
PA1 1HR

⚲ NS 488 642

⛪ Roman Catholic

🌐 www.paisleydiocese.org.uk

Built in 1931 to replace the old church in East Buchanan Street. Constituted Cathedral Church of the Diocese of Paisley in 1947. The architect was Thomas Baird, and the building is neo-Romanesque in style with an airy arched interior. Sculpted pulpit and Art Deco Stations of the Cross.

- Sunday: 8.00am, 10.00am and 12.00 noon; weekdays: 10.00am and 1.00pm
- Open daily 8.00am–8.00pm (0141-889 2404)

104 CASTLEHEAD PARISH CHURCH, PAISLEY

Main Road
Castlehead
Paisley
PA2 6AH

⚲ NS 476 636

⛪ Church of Scotland

Junction with Canal Street

Built 1781 as the first Relief Church in Paisley. Simple but dignified building with lancet windows. Interior renovated 1881. Bishop organ, 1898. Graveyard has graves of Robert Tannahill (local poet), past ministers, merchants and the mass graves of the 1823 cholera epidemic.

- Sunday: 11.00am
- Open May to September, Monday, Wednesday and Friday, 2.00–4.00pm (0141-889 7377)

105 ST JAMES'S CHURCH, PAISLEY

**Underwood Road
Paisley
PA3 1TL**

NS 477 644

Church of Scotland

Early French Gothic style to a design by Hippolyte Blanc, largely gifted by Sir Peter Coats, 1884. Spire 60 metres (200ft). Full peal of bells, rung every Sunday. 'Father' Willis pipe organ, rebuilt J. Walker, 1967. Stained-glass windows, 1904. Landscaped grounds.

- Sunday: 11.00am
- Open Monday, Wednesday and Friday, 10.00am–4.00pm (0141-889 1838)

106 THOMAS COATS MEMORIAL BAPTIST CHURCH, PAISLEY

**High Street
Paisley
PA1 2BA**

NS 478 640

Baptist

www.fenet.co.uk/coats

Built by the Coats family as a memorial to Thomas Coats. Designed by Hippolyte Blanc in Gothic style, opened May 1894. Cathedral-like with a crown steeple, and given extra prominence by a wide and high flight of steps to the main door. Beautiful interior, with carved marble and alabaster. Famous Hill 4-manual pipe organ.

- Sunday: 11.00am
- Open Friday 2.00–4.00pm May to September; or by arrangement (0141-587 8992)

107 WALLNEUK NORTH CHURCH, PAISLEY

**Abercorn Street
Paisley
PA3 4AG**

⚔ NS 486 643

⛪ Church of Scotland

🌐 www.wallneuknorthchurch.co.uk

Built 1915 in Arts & Crafts Gothic by architect T. G. Abercrombie. Tall nave and tower in red sandstone. Pipe organ by Abbott & Smith of Leeds, 1931, dedicated to Peter Coats, donor of this church. Its fine oak case was carved and built by Wylie & Lochhead, Glasgow.

- Sunday: 11.00am; Wednesday: 12.30pm
- Open by arrangement (0141-889 9265)

 (by arrangement)

 (by arrangement)

108 PAISLEY MARTYRS' SANDYFORD CHURCH

Martyrs' Church

**Broomlands Street
Paisley
PA1 2LS**

⚔ NS 474 639

⛪ Church of Scotland

The church is named after the Paisley Martyrs who were executed in 1685. Built 1847 with additions and alterations, including tower and south front in neo-Norman style, 1905; T. G. Abercrombie, architect. Inside are galleries on three sides on cast-iron columns. The pulpit, 5.5 metres (18ft) long, has been likened to the bridge of a ship.

- Sunday: 11.00am
- Open Friday 10.00am–1.00pm (0141-889 6603)

 (Friday 10.00am–1.00pm)

109 **NEW JERUSALEM CHURCH, PAISLEY**

17 George Street
Paisley
PA1 2LB

 NS 481 637

Swedenborgian

🌐 www.paisleynewchurch.org.uk

Built for Wesleyan Methodists in 1810, and in use by Swedenborgians since 1860, the building has halls on the ground floor and the church upstairs. Three striking stained-glass windows by W. & J. J. Keir, including one designed by Sir Noel Paton. Fine pulpit, communion table and ceiling rose.

- Sunday: 11.00am
- Open by arrangement (0141-581 0864)

110 **ST MARY'S (OUR LADY HELP OF CHRISTIANS), PAISLEY**

167 George Street
Paisley
PA1 2UN

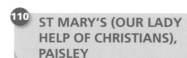 NS 471 636

Roman Catholic

Designed by Pugin & Pugin in Decorated Gothic style and built 1891; apse added 1905. Organ by Andrew of Glasgow. Recent refurbishment has included redecoration of the interior. The church contains works of Austrian and Bavarian origin.

- Saturday: 6.30pm; Sunday: 9.30am and 11.00am; Monday, Tuesday, Friday and Saturday: 9.30am; Wednesday: 7.00pm
- Open daily 8.30am–12.30pm (0141-889 2602)

111 ST PETER'S, PAISLEY

154 Braehead Road
Paisley
PA2 8NG

A NS 474 613

🏠 Roman Catholic

🌐 www.stpeterspaisley.org.uk

The church, with its brick tower, is a dominant feature on the hill at Glenburn. It was completed in 1958 and a new church hall opened in 2003.

- Saturday: 9.30am and 6.30pm; Sunday: 10.00am, 12.00 noon and 5.15pm; Monday to Friday: 9.30am; Wednesday: 7.00pm
- Open by arrangement (0141-884 2435)

112 OAKSHAW TRINITY CHURCH, PAISLEY

Oakshaw Street
Paisley
PA1 2DD

A NS 480 641

🏠 Church of Scotland, United Reformed Church

🌐 www.oakshawtrinity.org.uk

Top of Church Hill at Oakshaw Street East

Former Paisley High Church, built 1756 by John White; the steeple added 1770; renovated and extended during the 19th century. A rectangular classical church with galleried interior, the organ set under the tower. Stained glass by Ballantine & Sons.

- Sunday: 11.00am
- Open by arrangement (0141-887 4647)

113 ST CHARLES, PAISLEY

**5 Union Street
Paisley
PA2 6DU**

NS 483 633

Roman Catholic

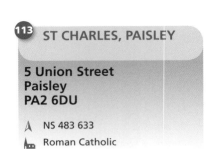

The parish of St Charles was established in 1897 and had three churches, the present occupying the site of the original. Designed by J. G. Quigley, 1986, it forms a courtyard enclosure with the hall and presbytery. Predominantly top-lit, it has a bright and spacious interior. The altar was built from the altar used by Pope John Paul II at Bellahouston in 1982.

- Saturday: 7.00pm; Sunday: 10.30am, 12.00 noon and 7.00pm; weekdays: 10.00am
- Open daily 9.00am–5.00pm (0141-889 2614)

114 GLASGOW INTERNATIONAL AIRPORT CHAPEL

**Glasgow Airport
Paisley
PA3 2SW**

NS 478 663

Non-denominational

Linked with Renfrew Old (116)

Second floor of terminal building

Simple space for prayer and contemplation, open to passengers and staff of all faiths and creeds.

- Services are announced 30 minutes in advance by public address
- Open at all times (0141-886 2005)

115 ST MACHAR'S, RANFURLY

**Kilbarchan Road
Ranfurly
PA11 3EG**

NS 392 653

Church of Scotland

www.stmacharsranfurly.org

East end of village

Early Gothic church of 1878 by Lewis Shanks, brother of one of the local mill-owners. The chancel was added in 1910 by Alexander Hislop. Outstanding stained glass by J. S. Melville & J. Stewart, 1900, Herbert Hendrie, 1931, William Wilson, 1946, and Gordon Webster, 1956.

- Sunday: 11.00am (10.30am July and August)
- Open Friday 10.00am–12.00 noon (01505 613447)

116 RENFREW OLD PARISH CHURCH

**26 High Street
Renfrew
PA4 8QR**

NS 509 676

Church of Scotland

Linked with Glasgow Airport Chapel (114)

The Church of Renfrew was bestowed by King David on the Cathedral Church of Glasgow in 1136. The present church, in early Gothic style, was built in 1861–2 and designed by John Thomas Rochead. The chancel was remodelled by Peter Macgregor Chalmers in 1908. Reredos of 1937 by Waddell & Young. Two late medieval monuments in the chancel.

- Sunday: 11.15am and 6.30pm
- Open by arrangement (0141-886 2005)

117 ST MUNGO'S, ALEXANDRIA

Main Street
Alexandria
G83 0BN

⚔ NS 389 796

⛪ Scottish Episcopal

🌐 www.stmungos.net

Dedicated 1894, by J. M. Crawford, architect, in pointed Gothic style. Simple interior with plain altar furniture. Three-light stained-glass window in memory of Agnes J. Burham of New York, featuring Christ in Majesty, St Michael the Archangel, St Agnes and St Agatha.

- Sunday: 9.00am and 11.00am; Wednesday: 10.00am
- Open by arrangement (01389 752633)

118 ALEXANDRIA PARISH CHURCH

Lomond Road
Balloch
G83 8SJ

⚔ NS 387 817

⛪ Church of Scotland

🌐 www.alexandriaparishchurch. co.uk

Off A82

1960s building refurbished and upgraded 1995–6. Digital organ by Allen. Tapestry, finely embroidered pulpit falls, communion table cords, and banners by local embroiderers. Several noteworthy items of stained glass. Noah's Ark mural in main hall.

- Sunday: 11.00am all year and 9.30am mid-June to end August
- Open by arrangement (01389 751143)

 (by arrangement)

119 KILBOWIE ST ANDREW'S PARISH CHURCH, CLYDEBANK

**Kilbowie Road
Clydebank
G81 1TH**

NS 499 712

Church of Scotland

Junction with Drumry Road

Built 1904, on land gifted by William Black of Auchentoshen, in simple Perpendicular style; battlemented belfry added 1933. Memorial side chapel with tapestry and stained-glass window by Eilidh Keith, 1997, dedicated to the victims of the Clydebank Blitz. The bell of 1933 is one of few remaining in this former industrial community of Scotland.

- Sunday: 11.00am, except July and August
- Open by arrangement (0141-951 2455)

120 ST JOSEPH'S, FAIFLEY, CLYDEBANK

**281 Faifley Road
Clydebank
G81 5EZ**

NS 510 733

Roman Catholic

Replacing a Coia church which was burned down, the building was opened in 1997. The award-winning design by Jacobsen & French utilises tall windows to provide light, while natural wood is featured extensively.

- Saturday: 6.00pm; Sunday: 11.00am; daily Mass: 9.30am
- Open Wednesday 9.00–11.00am, Saturday 5.00–7.15pm, Sunday 9.00am–12.30pm (01389 872236)

121 ST PATRICK'S, DUMBARTON

**Strathleven Place
Dumbarton
G82 1BA**

⚐ NS 399 755

⛪ Roman Catholic

🌐 www.stpatricksdumbarton.org.uk

An elegant red sandstone building by Dunn and Hansom, completed in 1903. It was enhanced in 1926–7 with a fine tower by Pugin & Pugin and carillon of bells. The sanctuary was extended in 1935 and reordered in 1997 to make it compatible with the renewed liturgy of the Eucharist.

- Saturday: 6.30pm; Sunday: 10.00am, 12.00 noon and 5.30pm
- Open daily from 8.00am until evening, 4.00pm in winter (01389 762503)

122 THE CHURCH OF KILMARONOCK

**Drymen
G83 8SB**

⚐ NS 452 875

⛪ Church of Scotland

North side of A811, 5km (3 miles) west of Drymen

Parish long established when documented records began; screen at entrance to nave lists incumbents since 1325. The present church building dates from 1813 and has a stout classical dignity. Memorial wall plaques. Ancient stones in graveyard.

- Sunday: 11.00am, May to September
- Open by arrangement (01360 660295)

123 RIVERSIDE PARISH CHURCH, DUMBARTON

High Street
Dumbarton
G82 1NB

Ⓐ NS 398 752

🏛 Church of Scotland

🌐 www.dumbartonriverside.org.uk

Built in 1811 to a design by John Brash on the site of earlier churches. The steeple commands the westward curve of the High Street. The interior was refurbished in 1886. Stained glass by the Abbey Studio of Glasgow and C. E. Stewart. Spectacular millennium window by John Clark, 2002. Crusader stone of 11th/12th century now housed in gallery.

* Sunday: 11.15am
* Open weekdays 9.30am–12.30pm (01389 742551)

124 ST AUGUSTINE'S, DUMBARTON

High Street
Dumbarton
G82 1LL

Ⓐ NS 397 752

🏛 Scottish Episcopal

🌐 www.staugustinesdumbarton.co.uk

Gothic Revival church by Robert Rowand Anderson. Stained glass at baptismal font by Stephen Adam, with others by Carl Alnquist. The organ was designed and built for the church by Smith and Brock. Total restoration of building, 2003.

* Sunday: 9.00am and 11.00am
* Open Saturday mornings or by arrangement (01389 734514)

WEST DUNBARTONSHIRE

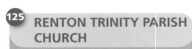

125 RENTON TRINITY PARISH CHURCH

**Alexander Street
Renton
G82 4LT**

A NS 390 780

Church of Scotland

Building originally constructed as
Renton Old Parish Church, 1892,
architects H. & D. Barclay. United with
Renton Union Church and Renton
Millburn Church, 1969. Has since
been refurbished and upgraded.
Five stained-glass windows by Oscar
Paterson, Glasgow, 1912–22.

- Sunday: 11.30am
- Open by arrangement (01389 752017)

Index

References are to each church's entry number in the gazetteer.